Florida

State Assessments
Grade 8 Science

SUCCESS STRATEGIES

FSA Test Review for the
Florida Standards Assessments

Dear Future Exam Success Story:

First of all, **THANK YOU** for purchasing Mometrix study materials!

Second, congratulations! You are one of the few determined test-takers who are committed to doing whatever it takes to excel on your exam. **You have come to the right place.** We developed these study materials with one goal in mind: to deliver you the information you need in a format that's concise and easy to use.

In addition to optimizing your guide for the content of the test, we've outlined our recommended steps for breaking down the preparation process into small, attainable goals so you can make sure you stay on track.

We've also analyzed the entire test-taking process, identifying the most common pitfalls and showing how you can overcome them and be ready for any curveball the test throws you.

Standardized testing is one of the biggest obstacles on your road to success, which only increases the importance of doing well in the high-pressure, high-stakes environment of test day. Your results on this test could have a significant impact on your future, and this guide provides the information and practical advice to help you achieve your full potential on test day.

Your success is our success

We would love to hear from you! If you would like to share the story of your exam success or if you have any questions or comments in regard to our products, please contact us at **800-673-8175** or **support@mometrix.com**.

Thanks again for your business and we wish you continued success!

Sincerely,
The Mometrix Test Preparation Team

Need more help? Check out our flashcards at: http://mometrixflashcards.com/FSA

TABLE OF CONTENTS

Introduction

Thank you for purchasing this resource! You have made the choice to prepare yourself for a test that could have a huge impact on your future, and this guide is designed to help you be fully ready for test day. Obviously, it's important to have a solid understanding of the test material, but you also need to be prepared for the unique environment and stressors of the test, so that you can perform to the best of your abilities.

For this purpose, the first section that appears in this guide is the **Success Strategies**. We've devoted countless hours to meticulously researching what works and what doesn't, and we've boiled down our findings to the five most impactful steps you can take to improve your performance on the test. We start at the beginning with study planning and move through the preparation process, all the way to the testing strategies that will help you get the most out of what you know when you're finally sitting in front of the test.

We recommend that you start preparing for your test as far in advance as possible. However, if you've bought this guide as a last-minute study resource and only have a few days before your test, we recommend that you skip over the first two Success Strategies since they address a long-term study plan.

If you struggle with **test anxiety**, we strongly encourage you to check out our recommendations for how you can overcome it. Test anxiety is a formidable foe, but it can be beaten, and we want to make sure you have the tools you need to defeat it.

Success Strategy #1 – Plan Big, Study Small

There's a lot riding on your performance. If you want to ace this test, you're going to need to keep your skills sharp and the material fresh in your mind. You need a plan that lets you review everything you need to know while still fitting in your schedule. We'll break this strategy down into three categories.

Information Organization

Start with the information you already have: the official test outline. From this, you can make a complete list of all the concepts you need to cover before the test. Organize these concepts into groups that can be studied together, and create a list of any related vocabulary you need to learn so you can brush up on any difficult terms. You'll want to keep this vocabulary list handy once you actually start studying since you may need to add to it along the way.

Time Management

Once you have your set of study concepts, decide how to spread them out over the time you have left before the test. Break your study plan into small, clear goals so you have a manageable task for each day and know exactly what you're doing. Then just focus on one small step at a time. When you manage your time this way, you don't need to spend hours at a time studying. Studying a small block of content for a short period each day helps you retain information better and avoid stressing over how much you have left to do. You can relax knowing that you have a plan to cover everything in time. In order for this strategy to be effective though, you have to start studying early and stick to your schedule. Avoid the exhaustion and futility that comes from last-minute cramming!

Study Environment

The environment you study in has a big impact on your learning. Studying in a coffee shop, while probably more enjoyable, is not likely to be as fruitful as studying in a quiet room. It's important to keep distractions to a minimum. You're only planning to study for a short block of time, so make the most of it. Don't pause to check your phone or get up to find a snack. It's also important to **avoid multitasking**. Research has consistently shown that multitasking will make your studying dramatically less effective. Your study area should also be comfortable and well-lit so you don't have the distraction of straining your eyes or sitting on an uncomfortable chair.

The time of day you study is also important. You want to be rested and alert. Don't wait until just before bedtime. Study when you'll be most likely to comprehend and remember. Even better, if you know what time of day your test will be, set that time aside for study. That way your brain will be used to working on that subject at that specific time and you'll have a better chance of recalling information.

Finally, it can be helpful to team up with others who are studying for the same test. Your actual studying should be done in as isolated an environment as possible, but the work of organizing the information and setting up the study plan can be divided up. In between study sessions, you can discuss with your teammates the concepts that you're all studying and quiz each other on the details. Just be sure that your teammates are as serious about the test as you are. If you find that your study time is being replaced with social time, you might need to find a new team.

Success Strategy #2 – Make Your Studying Count

You're devoting a lot of time and effort to preparing for this test, so you want to be absolutely certain it will pay off. This means doing more than just reading the content and hoping you can remember it on test day. It's important to make every minute of study count. There are two main areas you can focus on to make your studying count:

Retention

It doesn't matter how much time you study if you can't remember the material. You need to make sure you are retaining the concepts. To check your retention of the information you're learning, try recalling it at later times with minimal prompting. Try carrying around flashcards and glance at one or two from time to time or ask a friend who's also studying for the test to quiz you.

To enhance your retention, look for ways to put the information into practice so that you can apply it rather than simply recalling it. If you're using the information in practical ways, it will be much easier to remember. Similarly, it helps to solidify a concept in your mind if you're not only reading it to yourself but also explaining it to someone else. Ask a friend to let you teach them about a concept you're a little shaky on (or speak aloud to an imaginary audience if necessary). As you try to summarize, define, give examples, and answer your friend's questions, you'll understand the concepts better and they will stay with you longer. Finally, step back for a big picture view and ask yourself how each piece of information fits with the whole subject. When you link the different concepts together and see them working together as a whole, it's easier to remember the individual components.

Finally, practice showing your work on any multi-step problems, even if you're just studying. Writing out each step you take to solve a problem will help solidify the process in your mind, and you'll be more likely to remember it during the test.

Modality

Modality simply refers to the means or method by which you study. Choosing a study modality that fits your own individual learning style is crucial. No two people learn best in exactly the same way, so it's important to know your strengths and use them to your advantage.

For example, if you learn best by visualization, focus on visualizing a concept in your mind and draw an image or a diagram. Try color-coding your notes, illustrating them, or creating symbols that will trigger your mind to recall a learned concept. If you learn best by hearing or discussing information, find a study partner who learns the same way or read aloud to yourself. Think about how to put the information in your own words. Imagine that you are giving a lecture on the topic and record yourself so you can listen to it later.

For any learning style, flashcards can be helpful. Organize the information so you can take advantage of spare moments to review. Underline key words or phrases. Use different colors for different categories. Mnemonic devices (such as creating a short list in which every item starts with the same letter) can also help with retention. Find what works best for you and use it to store the information in your mind most effectively and easily.

Success Strategy #3 – Practice the Right Way

Your success on test day depends not only on how many hours you put into preparing, but also on whether you prepared the right way. It's good to check along the way to see if your studying is paying off. One of the most effective ways to do this is by taking practice tests to evaluate your progress. Practice tests are useful because they show exactly where you need to improve. Every time you take a practice test, pay special attention to these three groups of questions:

- The questions you got wrong
- The questions you had to guess on, even if you guessed right
- The questions you found difficult or slow to work through

This will show you exactly what your weak areas are, and where you need to devote more study time. Ask yourself why each of these questions gave you trouble. Was it because you didn't understand the material? Was it because you didn't remember the vocabulary? Do you need more repetitions on this type of question to build speed and confidence? Dig into those questions and figure out how you can strengthen your weak areas as you go back to review the material.

Additionally, many practice tests have a section explaining the answer choices. It can be tempting to read the explanation and think that you now have a good understanding of the concept. However, an explanation likely only covers part of the question's broader context. Even if the explanation makes sense, **go back and investigate** every concept related to the question until you're positive you have a thorough understanding.

As you go along, keep in mind that the practice test is just that: practice. Memorizing these questions and answers will not be very helpful on the actual test because it is unlikely to have any of the same exact questions. If you only know the right answers to the sample questions, you won't be prepared for the real thing. **Study the concepts** until you understand them fully, and then you'll be able to answer any question that shows up on the test.

It's important to wait on the practice tests until you're ready. If you take a test on your first day of study, you may be overwhelmed by the amount of material covered and how much you need to learn. Work up to it gradually.

On test day, you'll need to be prepared for answering questions, managing your time, and using the test-taking strategies you've learned. It's a lot to balance, like a mental marathon that will have a big impact on your future. Like training for a marathon, you'll need to start slowly and work your way up. When test day arrives, you'll be ready.

Start with what you've read in the first two Success Strategies—plan your course and study in the way that works best for you. If you have time, consider using multiple study resources to get different approaches to the same concepts. It can be helpful to see difficult concepts from more than one angle. Then find a good source for practice tests. Many times, the test website will suggest potential study resources or provide sample tests.

Practice Test Strategy

When you're ready to start taking practice tests, follow this strategy:

Untimed and Open-Book Practice

Take the first test with no time constraints and with your notes and study guide handy. Take your time and focus on applying the strategies you've learned.

Timed and Open-Book Practice

Take the second practice test open-book as well, but set a timer and practice pacing yourself to finish in time.

Timed and Closed-Book Practice

Take any other practice tests as if it were test day. Set a timer and put away your study materials. Sit at a table or desk in a quiet room, imagine yourself at the testing center, and answer questions as quickly and accurately as possible.

Keep repeating timed and closed-book tests on a regular basis until you run out of practice tests or it's time for the actual test. Your mind will be ready for the schedule and stress of test day, and you'll be able to focus on recalling the material you've learned.

Success Strategy #4 – Pace Yourself

Once you're fully prepared for the material on the test, your biggest challenge on test day will be managing your time. Just knowing that the clock is ticking can make you panic even if you have plenty of time left. Work on pacing yourself so you can build confidence against the time constraints of the exam. Pacing is a difficult skill to master, especially in a high-pressure environment, so **practice is vital**.

Set time expectations for your pace based on how much time is available. For example, if a section has 60 questions and the time limit is 30 minutes, you know you have to average 30 seconds or less per question in order to answer them all. Although 30 seconds is the hard limit, set 25 seconds per question as your goal, so you reserve extra time to spend on harder questions. When you budget extra time for the harder questions, you no longer have any reason to stress when those questions take longer to answer.

Don't let this time expectation distract you from working through the test at a calm, steady pace, but keep it in mind so you don't spend too much time on any one question. Recognize that taking extra time on one question you don't understand may keep you from answering two that you do understand later in the test. If your time limit for a question is up and you're still not sure of the answer, mark it and move on, and come back to it later if the time and the test format allow. If the testing format doesn't allow you to return to earlier questions, just make an educated guess; then put it out of your mind and move on.

On the easier questions, be careful not to rush. It may seem wise to hurry through them so you have more time for the challenging ones, but it's not worth missing one if you know the concept and just didn't take the time to read the question fully. Work efficiently but make sure you understand the question and have looked at all of the answer choices, since more than one may seem right at first.

Even if you're paying attention to the time, you may find yourself a little behind at some point. You should speed up to get back on track, but do so wisely. Don't panic; just take a few seconds less on each question until you're caught up. Don't guess without thinking, but do look through the answer choices and eliminate any you know are wrong. If you can get down to two choices, it is often worthwhile to guess from those. Once you've chosen an answer, move on and don't dwell on any that you skipped or had to hurry through. If a question was taking too long, chances are it was one of the harder ones, so you weren't as likely to get it right anyway.

On the other hand, if you find yourself getting ahead of schedule, it may be beneficial to slow down a little. The more quickly you work, the more likely you are to make a careless mistake that will affect your score. You've budgeted time for each question, so don't be afraid to spend that time. Practice an efficient but careful pace to get the most out of the time you have.

Test-Taking Strategies

This section contains a list of test-taking strategies that you may find helpful as you work through the test. By taking what you know and applying logical thought, you can maximize your chances of answering any question correctly!

It is very important to realize that every question is different and every person is different: no single strategy will work on every question, and no single strategy will work for every person. That's why we've included all of them here, so you can try them out and determine which ones work best for different types of questions and which ones work best for you.

Question Strategies

Read Carefully

Read the question and answer choices carefully. Don't miss the question because you misread the terms. You have plenty of time to read each question thoroughly and make sure you understand what is being asked. Yet a happy medium must be attained, so don't waste too much time. You must read carefully, but efficiently.

Contextual Clues

Look for contextual clues. If the question includes a word you are not familiar with, look at the immediate context for some indication of what the word might mean. Contextual clues can often give you all the information you need to decipher the meaning of an unfamiliar word. Even if you can't determine the meaning, you may be able to narrow down the possibilities enough to make a solid guess at the answer to the question.

Prefixes

If you're having trouble with a word in the question or answer choices, try dissecting it. Take advantage of every clue that the word might include. Prefixes and suffixes can be a huge help. Usually they allow you to determine a basic meaning. Pre- means before, post- means after, pro - is positive, de- is negative. From prefixes and suffixes, you can get an idea of the general meaning of the word and try to put it into context.

Hedge Words

Watch out for critical hedge words, such as *likely, may, can, sometimes, often, almost, mostly, usually, generally, rarely,* and *sometimes*. Question writers insert these hedge phrases to cover every possibility. Often an answer choice will be wrong simply because it leaves no room for exception. Be on guard for answer choices that have definitive words such as *exactly* and *always*.

Switchback Words

Stay alert for *switchbacks*. These are the words and phrases frequently used to alert you to shifts in thought. The most common switchback words are *but, although,* and *however*. Others include *nevertheless, on the other hand, even though, while, in spite of, despite, regardless of*. Switchback words are important to catch because they can change the direction of the question or an answer choice.

Face Value

When in doubt, use common sense. Accept the situation in the problem at face value. Don't read too much into it. These problems will not require you to make wild assumptions. If you have to go beyond creativity and warp time or space in order to have an answer choice fit the question, then you should move on and consider the other answer choices. These are normal problems rooted in reality. The applicable relationship or explanation may not be readily apparent, but it is there for you to figure out. Use your common sense to interpret anything that isn't clear.

Answer Choice Strategies

Answer Selection

The most thorough way to pick an answer choice is to identify and eliminate wrong answers until only one is left, then confirm it is the correct answer. Sometimes an answer choice may immediately seem right, but be careful. The test writers will usually put more than one reasonable answer choice on each question, so take a second to read all of them and make sure that the other choices are not equally obvious. As long as you have time left, it is better to read every answer choice than to pick the first one that looks right without checking the others.

Answer Choice Families

An answer choice family consists of two (in rare cases, three) answer choices that are very similar in construction and cannot all be true at the same time. If you see two answer choices that are direct opposites or parallels, one of them is usually the correct answer. For instance, if one answer choice says that quantity x increases and another either says that quantity x decreases (opposite) or says that quantity y increases (parallel), then those answer choices would fall into the same family. An answer choice that doesn't match the construction of the answer choice family is more likely to be incorrect. Most questions will not have answer choice families, but when they do appear, you should be prepared to recognize them.

Eliminate Answers

Eliminate answer choices as soon as you realize they are wrong, but make sure you consider all possibilities. If you are eliminating answer choices and realize that the last one you are left with is also wrong, don't panic. Start over and consider each choice again. There may be something you missed the first time that you will realize on the second pass.

Avoid Fact Traps

Don't be distracted by an answer choice that is factually true but doesn't answer the question. You are looking for the choice that answers the question. Stay focused on what the question is asking for so you don't accidentally pick an answer that is true but incorrect. Always go back to the question and make sure the answer choice you've selected actually answers the question and is not merely a true statement.

Extreme Statements

In general, you should avoid answers that put forth extreme actions as standard practice or proclaim controversial ideas as established fact. An answer choice that states the "process should be used in certain situations, if..." is much more likely to be correct than one that states the "process should be discontinued completely." The first is a calm rational statement and doesn't even make a

- 8 -

definitive, uncompromising stance, using a hedge word *if* to provide wiggle room, whereas the second choice is a radical idea and far more extreme.

Benchmark

As you read through the answer choices and you come across one that seems to answer the question well, mentally select that answer choice. This is not your final answer, but it's the one that will help you evaluate the other answer choices. The one that you selected is your benchmark or standard for judging each of the other answer choices. Every other answer choice must be compared to your benchmark. That choice is correct until proven otherwise by another answer choice beating it. If you find a better answer, then that one becomes your new benchmark. Once you've decided that no other choice answers the question as well as your benchmark, you have your final answer.

Predict the Answer

Before you even start looking at the answer choices, it is often best to try to predict the answer. When you come up with the answer on your own, it is easier to avoid distractions and traps because you will know exactly what to look for. The right answer choice is unlikely to be word-for-word what you came up with, but it should be a close match. Even if you are confident that you have the right answer, you should still take the time to read each option before moving on.

General Strategies

Tough Questions

If you are stumped on a problem or it appears too hard or too difficult, don't waste time. Move on! Remember though, if you can quickly check for obviously incorrect answer choices, your chances of guessing correctly are greatly improved. Before you completely give up, at least try to knock out a couple of possible answers. Eliminate what you can and then guess at the remaining answer choices before moving on.

Check Your Work

Since you will probably not know every term listed and the answer to every question, it is important that you get credit for the ones that you do know. Don't miss any questions through careless mistakes. If at all possible, try to take a second to look back over your answer selection and make sure you've selected the correct answer choice and haven't made a costly careless mistake (such as marking an answer choice that you didn't mean to mark). This quick double check should more than pay for itself in caught mistakes for the time it costs.

Pace Yourself

It's easy to be overwhelmed when you're looking at a page full of questions; your mind is confused and full of random thoughts, and the clock is ticking down faster than you would like. Calm down and maintain the pace that you have set for yourself. Especially as you get down to the last few minutes of the test, don't let the small numbers on the clock make you panic. As long as you are on track by monitoring your pace, you are guaranteed to have time for each question.

Don't Rush

It is very easy to make errors when you are in a hurry. Maintaining a fast pace in answering questions is pointless if it makes you miss questions that you would have gotten right otherwise. Test writers like to include distracting information and wrong answers that seem right. Taking a little extra time to avoid careless mistakes can make all the difference in your test score. Find a pace that allows you to be confident in the answers that you select.

Keep Moving

Panicking will not help you pass the test, so do your best to stay calm and keep moving. Taking deep breaths and going through the answer elimination steps you practiced can help to break through a stress barrier and keep your pace.

Final Notes

The combination of a solid foundation of content knowledge and the confidence that comes from practicing your plan for applying that knowledge is the key to maximizing your performance on test day. As your foundation of content knowledge is built up and strengthened, you'll find that the strategies included in this chapter become more and more effective in helping you quickly sift through the distractions and traps of the test to isolate the correct answer.

Now it's time to move on to the test content chapters of this book, but be sure to keep your goal in mind. As you read, think about how you will be able to apply this information on the test. If you've already seen sample questions for the test and you have an idea of the question format and style, try to come up with questions of your own that you can answer based on what you're reading. This will give you valuable practice applying your knowledge in the same ways you can expect to on test day.

Good luck and good studying!

Physical Sciences

Structure of an atom

A neutral atom consists of an extremely dense nucleus composed of one or more positively charged protons and (except for hydrogen-1) a varying number of uncharged neutrons. The nucleus is surrounded by a cloud of one or more negatively charged electrons that are equal in number to the protons in the nucleus. The protons and neutrons are bound together by the strong nuclear force, which is stronger than the repulsive force between the positively charged protons. The negatively charged electrons are attracted to the positively charged protons by the electromagnetic force. The number of protons determines the identity of the chemical element, while the number of electrons in the outermost shell determines the ways in which the atom interacts chemically with other atoms or molecules.

Chemical compound

A chemical compound consists of two or more different elements with a fixed ratio of atoms. These atoms are held in a specific arrangement by covalent, ionic, or metallic bonds. Substances formed from two or more atoms of a single element are not considered compounds. Examples are diatomic hydrogen, oxygen, nitrogen, and chlorine (H_2, O_2, N_2, Cl_2) or polyatomic molecules such as O_3 (ozone), P_4, and S_8. An example of a compound is when two hydrogen atoms and one oxygen atom combine to form water (H_2O). Other examples of compounds include: two hydrogen atoms, one sulfur atom, and four oxygen atoms combine to form sulfuric acid (H_2SO_4); two oxygen atoms and a carbon atom come together to make carbon dioxide (CO_2); and four hydrogen atoms and a carbon atom combine to form methane (CH_4).

Speed vs. velocity

Speed is a scalar quantity. That is, it has a magnitude but no direction. **Velocity** is a vector quantity so it has both magnitude and direction. For example, if you drive your car at a constant 70 kilometers per hour in any direction, you will be traveling at the same speed. Even if you drive around a curve and change your direction of travel, you are still traveling at the same speed as long as the car remains at 70 km/h. However, if you change your direction of travel, you have changed your velocity. Velocity is a specified speed in a specified direction. When you go around a corner in your car, even though you maintain the same speed, you have changed velocity. Any change in velocity, such as a change in speed, direction, or both, constitutes an **acceleration** and requires that a net unbalanced force act upon the moving system.

Newton's first two Laws of Motion

Newton's First Law of Motion states that an object at rest remains at rest and an object in motion remains in motion with the same speed and in the same direction, unless acted upon by a net unbalanced force. No change in acceleration occurs so $a = 0$ m/s^2. Newton's First Law is often called the law of inertia. Inertia is the natural tendency of all objects to resist any change in their state of motion. It is measured by an object's mass; the greater the mass, the greater the resistance to a change in motion. Newton's Second Law of Motion states that unbalanced force acting upon a body will produce a change in that body's acceleration that is directly proportional to the force applied and inversely proportional to the body's mass. The formula associated with Newton's Second law is $F_{net} = ma$. This equation states that the net force (F_{net}) applied to a body of mass m will produce an acceleration a in the same direction as the force applied.

Third Law of Motion

Newton's Third Law of Motion states that every action has an equal and opposite reaction. Whenever you exert an action, pushing on a wall, for example, there is a reaction. The wall pushes back directly against you with the same amount of force. The equal and opposite force exerted by the wall against your hands and arms is the resistance you feel. As long as your action and the wall's reaction are balanced, no net force is exerted and neither you nor the wall moves: $\overrightarrow{F}_1 = -\overleftarrow{F}_2$. However, if you replace the wall with a flimsy bamboo curtain, you can easily push it aside or knock it over. The bamboo curtain's inertia is not enough to counteract the force you apply and a net unbalanced force acts against it causing the curtain to move. In this case, Newton's Second Law applies to the bamboo curtain: $\overrightarrow{F}$ net = ma. Newton's Third Law is also what allows the downward thrust of a rocket's engine to launch a spaceship upward into space.

Newton's Third Law states that, for every force, there is an equal and opposite force that arises in response. When a hammer strikes a nail, the nail hits the hammer just as hard. If we consider two objects, A and B, then we may express any contact between these two bodies with the equation $F_{AB} = -F_{BA}$ where the order of the subscripts denotes which body is exerting the force. At first glance, this law might seem to forbid any movement at all since every force is being countered with an equal opposite force, but these equal opposite forces are acting on different bodies with different masses, so they will not cancel each other out.

Mass vs. weight

Mass is a measure of the amount of matter contained in an object. It is expressed in **kilograms** (kg) in the International System of Units (SI) system and **slugs** in the English (Imperial) system. For comparison, 1 kg = 0.068521765562 slug; and 1 slug = 14.5939 kg. An object's mass remains the same everywhere in the universe. A 70-kg man has the same mass on Earth, on the Moon, or in outer space. **Weight** is the force of gravity acting upon a body. It is expressed in **newtons** (N) in the SI system and **pounds** (lbs) in the Imperial system. A force of 1 newton will accelerate a mass of 1 kilogram by 1 meter per second every second: $1 \text{ N} = 1 \text{ kg} \cdot \text{m/s}^2$. Likewise, a force of 1 pound will accelerate a mass of 1 slug by 1 foot per second every second: $1 \text{ lb} = 1 \text{ slug} \cdot \text{ft/s}^2$. A major difference between mass and weight is that an object's weight changes depending on the force of gravity acting upon it. For example, a man that weighs 70 kilograms on Earth would only weigh about 12 kilograms on the Moon because there is less gravity on the Moon. On Jupiter, the man would weigh more than 165 kilograms because there is much more gravity there.

Centrifugal and centripetal forces

Centrifugal force is not really a force at all. It is simply inertia in action as described by Newton's First Law of Motion and applies to all bodies moving in a circle. Any object traveling in a circle or moving around a curve appears to experience an outward force pushing it away from the center of rotation or movement. It is not a force at all, but rather the object's inertial resistance to any change in its motion in a straight line. On the other hand, **centripetal force** is an actual force directed toward the center of an object's curving path of motion. For satellites orbiting a planet or planets orbiting the Sun, the centripetal force is provided by gravity. For an object swung around one's head at the end of a string, the centripetal force is due to the tension on the string.

Nonpolar covalent chemical bonds

Covalent bonds are formed when one or more pairs of electrons are shared between atoms. Two atoms with equal electronegativity will share the electron pairs equally. This results in a **nonpolar covalent bond** with a bond dipole moment of zero. This typically occurs when two nonmetals chemically bond together. The **octet rule** states that the outermost shell must contain 8 electrons to be complete. The exception is hydrogen and helium, which are complete with 2 electrons in the $1s$ orbital, Hydrogen, with a single electron in its valence ($1s$) shell, needs one more electron to be complete. By sharing electrons, two hydrogen atoms complete their valence shells to form diatomic hydrogen, H:H (H_2). Similarly, by equally sharing two pairs of electrons, 2 oxygen atoms form diatomic oxygen (O_2) with the Lewis structure O::O. Each oxygen atom now has a complete outer shell of 8 electrons. Both H_2 and O_2 exhibit nonpolar bonds because the atoms have equal electronegativities.

Isotopes

Most elements include atoms with varying numbers of neutrons and, therefore, differing atomic masses. These variants are called isotopes. This difference is reflected in the value given to the atomic mass number (A), which is the weighted average of all the naturally occurring isotopes of a given element. The standard atomic mass of carbon, 12.0107 amu (atomic mass units), reflects the relative proportion of about 99:1 for carbon's stable isotopes, $^{12}_{6}C$ and $^{13}_{6}C$. A radioactive form of carbon with two extra neutrons, $^{14}_{6}C$, is written out as "carbon-14," while the normal isotope, $^{12}_{6}C$, is written as "carbon-12." When carbon-14 undergoes beta-decay, one of its neutrons is changed into a proton plus an electron and an electron-antineutrino:

$$^{14}_{6}C \rightarrow {}^{14}_{7}N + e^- + \bar{\nu}_e$$

By gaining an extra proton, the carbon atom has transmuted into a nitrogen atom. Although the value of A can vary for a given element, the atomic number (Z) must remain the same or the atom becomes a different element entirely, as shown in the beta-decay of carbon-14.

Physical changes

Physical changes are those that alter a substance's appearance but do not affect the chemical properties of the substance. Changes in state are physical changes. A liquid can freeze into a solid, for example, or boil into a gas without changing the chemical nature of the substance. Ice, water vapor, and liquid water are all still water even though they are in different states of matter. Physical properties include such features as shape, texture, size, color, odor, volume, mass, and density. Some changes in color or odor can reflect physical changes, while others may indicate that a chemical change has occurred. Certain physical changes such as dissolving ionic or polar compounds in a solvent are actually considered to be physical changes, even though they involve the breaking of chemical bonds. However, if these solutions are allowed to evaporate, the original ionic solid will settle out as a precipitate so the chemical identity of the substance did not change. The line between physical and chemical changes is sometimes blurred.

Chemical changes

Chemical changes occur when chemical bonds are broken and new ones formed resulting in the creation of new substances that were previously not present. The original substances are transformed into new compounds or elements along with the release or absorption of energy. For example, methane can combine with oxygen to produce carbon dioxide, water, and energy in the following reaction: $CH_4 + 2\ O_2 \rightarrow CO_2 + 2\ H_2O$ + energy. Similarly, an acid and a base combine chemically to form a salt and water: $2\ NaOH + H_2SO_4 \rightarrow 2\ H_2O + Na_2SO_4$. The oxidation of iron (rusting) is a chemical change, as is the decomposition of water into oxygen and hydrogen when an electric current passes through the water:

$$2\ H_2O + electricity \rightarrow 2\ H_2 + O_2$$

Ionic bonds

Ionic bonds form when one or more electrons are transferred from one atom to another atom. This results in positively and negatively charged ions that then attract each other forming a bond. Ionic bonds usually occur when a metal and a nonmetal join together as with common table salt, NaCl. The strongly electronegative chlorine atom completely strips away the single valence electron of the sodium atom, resulting in a negatively charged chloride ion (Cl^-) and a positively charged sodium ion (Na^+). Sodium chloride (table salt) forms a dense crystal lattice in which the sodium cations and chloride anions are held together by the attraction between their electric charges.

Ionic compounds dissociate when placed in water. The slightly negative oxygen ends of the polar water molecules surround the positive sodium ions, while the positive hydrogen ends envelop the negative chloride ions. The attractive forces between the water molecule dipoles and the Na^+ and Cl^- ions of the salt crystal are stronger than the attraction between the sodium and chloride ions so the salt readily dissolves in water.

Formation of chemical compounds

A chemical compound consists of two or more different elements arranged in a fixed ratio of the atoms involved. These atoms are held in a specific structure by covalent, ionic, or metallic bonds. An example of a compound is water, which is made up of two hydrogen atoms and one oxygen atom (H_2O). Likewise, two hydrogen atoms, one sulfur atom, and four oxygen atoms combine to form sulfuric acid, H_2SO_4. Two oxygen atoms and a carbon atom come together to make carbon dioxide, CO_2; and four hydrogen atoms and a carbon atom combine to form methane, CH_4. Substances formed from two or more atoms of the same element are not considered to be compounds. Examples are diatomic hydrogen, oxygen, nitrogen, and chlorine (H_2, O_2, N_2, Cl_2) or polyatomic molecules like O_3 (ozone), P_4, and S_8.

Balancing chemical reactions (equations)

In a chemical equation, it is necessary to have the same number of atoms for each element on each side of the equation. Reactants appear on the left side of the equation and the products appear on the right. The elements are balanced by placing the necessary coefficients in front of each element or compound. In a simple example, diatomic hydrogen (H_2) combines with diatomic oxygen (O_2) to form water:

$$H2 + O2 \rightarrow H2O$$

Adding up all the atoms for each element shows that there is one more oxygen atom on the reactant side than the product side of the equation. Since water contains twice as many hydrogen atoms as oxygen atoms, placing the coefficient 2 in front of both the hydrogen molecule on the reactant side and the water molecule on the product side balances the equation:

$$2\ H2 + O2 \rightarrow 2\ H2O$$

Again, count the number of atoms of each element on both sides of the equation. There are 4 hydrogen atoms and 2 oxygen atoms on each side of the equation so it is balanced.

Molecule

A molecule is an electrically neutral combination of two or more atoms of the same or different elements joined by covalent bonds. Molecules can be as simple as diatomic hydrogen or oxygen (H_2 and O_2) or water (H_2O) to as complex as large biochemical macromolecules such as proteins, starches, and cellulose. Proteins can range in size from 50 to more than 2,000 amino acids linked by peptide bonds, while starches and cellulose molecules can consist of more than 10,000 smaller glucose molecules covalently linked together. Aggregations of polar molecules like water that join together temporarily by hydrogen bonds are not considered molecules, nor are electrically charged ions joined by ionic bonds. Metals, consisting of positively charged ions in a sea of delocalized electrons, are also not generally considered to be molecules.

Waves of electromagnetic radiation

Electromagnetic (E-M) radiation has both electric and magnetic wavelike components that oscillate perpendicular to both each other and to the direction the wave is traveling. Electromagnetic waves travel at the speed of light, which in a vacuum is approximately 3×10^8 m/s. As it passes through different media E-M radiation slows down and is refracted, or bent, depending on the medium it passes into. Both the frequency and energy of an E-M wave increase as the wavelength decreases. The energy of an E-M wave is given by $E = hf$ (sometimes written $E = h\nu$), where h = Planck's constant (6.62×10^{-34} J s) and f = the frequency in oscillations per second, or hertz (Hz).

Energy

Energy is the capacity to do work. Like mass, it is a scalar quantity having a numerical value associated with a unit, but no direction. In the International System of Units (SI), energy is measured in joules. One joule is the amount of energy used in applying a force of 1 Newton over a distance of 1 meter: $1\text{ J} = 1\text{ N} \bullet \text{m} = 1\text{ kg} \bullet \text{m}^2/\text{s}^2$. Energy can also be measured in watts, calories, several different British thermal units, and kilowatt-hours (for electricity), to name a few. Energy and mass may be converted from one form to the other in a proportion described by Einstein's famous equation, $E = mc^2$, where E = energy, m = the mass of an object, and c = the speed of light in a vacuum (approximately 3×10^8 m/s).

Ice floats in liquid water

Density is the mass (amount of matter) in a certain volume. The more matter there is, the more the object weighs. Most solids have more matter than the same volume of their liquids. This means that they are denser and sink in their own liquid. However, water is different. The molecules in ice are farther apart than they are in liquid water. That means that ice has less matter in it than the same volume of liquid water. Therefore, ice is less dense and floats in water.

Law of conservation of mass

The law of conservation of mass is also known as the law of conservation of matter. This basically means that in a closed system, the total mass of the products must equal the total mass of the reactants. This could also be stated that in a closed system, mass never changes. A consequence of this law is that matter is never created or destroyed during a typical chemical reaction. The atoms of the reactants are simply rearranged to form the products. The number and type of each specific atom involved in the reactants is identical to the number and type of atoms in the products. This is

- 16 -

the key principle used when balancing chemical equations. In a balanced chemical equation, the number of moles of each element on the reactant side equals the number of moles of each element on the product side.

Atomic number and atomic mass

The elements in the periodic table are arranged in order of increasing atomic number first left to right and then top to bottom across the periodic table. The atomic number represents the number of protons in the atoms of that element. Because of the increasing numbers of protons, the atomic mass typically also increases from left to right across a period and from top to bottom down a row. The atomic mass is a weighted average of all the naturally occurring isotopes of an element.

Chemical formulas

A chemical formula is a set of letters, numbers, and symbols that describe the elemental composition of a particular substance. Elements are listed by their periodic table symbol. A subscript number after the element symbol indicates the number of that type of element's atoms in the formula. If there is no subscript, there is only one atom of that type of element.

There are three common types of chemical formulas to be familiar with:

1. The *molecular formula* describes the elemental composition of a single molecule of a substance. For instance, the molecular formula for glucose is $C_6H_{12}O_6$, because each molecule of glucose contains six atoms of carbon and oxygen, and twelve atoms of hydrogen.
2. The *empirical formula* is a reduced form of the molecular formula that gives only the ratios of the elements in a substance. For instance, the empirical formula for glucose is CH_2O, because the ratio of carbon to hydrogen to oxygen in glucose is 1 to 2 to 1. The empirical formula will be the same as the molecular formula for many simple substances.
3. The *structural formula* is an expanded formula that gives information about the way that the atoms in a molecule are bonded. Below is an example of the structural formula for ethane:

$$H-\overset{\displaystyle \underset{|}{\overset{|}{H}}}{C}-\overset{\displaystyle \underset{|}{\overset{|}{H}}}{C}-H$$

Life Sciences

Phyletic gradualism vs. punctuated equilibrium

Phyletic gradualism is a hypothesis that explains the pattern of evolution. It states that natural selection proceeds in a steady, slow, continuous accumulation of adaptations that produces gradual, progressive, morphological changes *in the general population* that ultimately give rise to new species. This is "evolution by creeps" in which the entire parent population slowly changes into the descendant species. Supporters of phyletic gradualism counteract that lack of any intermediate ancestors in the fossil record by arguing that the fossil record is incomplete. In contrast, **punctuated equilibrium** is more "evolution by jerks". It states that species arise not as the gradual stepwise evolution of an entire population, but rather when a small segment of a population becomes physically or genetically isolated and undergoes rapid changes that result in a new species. The descendent population breaks off from the larger population, which remains largely unchanged. Long periods of no evolutionary change are punctuated by rapid events resulting in new species. Punctuate equilibrium could explain why the fossil record lacks any intermediate species.

Plants the capture and digest animals

While deriving most of their energy from photosynthesis, a number of plants also capture, kill, and digest animals and other organisms ranging from protozoans to invertebrates and even small vertebrates. Sundews, pitcher plants, and Venus flytraps are the best known of these carnivorous plants. They tend to live in acidic environments that are poor in nutrients, especially nitrogen. Aquatic bladderworts of the genus *Utricularia* capture prey using unique bladder traps attached to delicate branches. Water is constantly pumped out of the bladder by an active ion transport process, which produces a partial vacuum. When an aquatic invertebrate like *Daphnia* (water flea) brushes against the hairlike triggers on the outside of the bladder, a door to the vacuum is suddenly opened causing water to rush in sucking in the hapless prey with it. This can occur in less than $1/60$ of a second. The door is quickly slammed shut again and the animal is digested by the plant.

Prokaryotic vs. eukaryotic cells

Prokaryotic cells are generally smaller than eukaryotic cells, lack a membrane-bound nucleus or membrane-bound organelles, and possess a single-stranded, circular DNA molecule that is free-floating in the cytoplasm. They have internal structures, such as ribosomes, centrioles, often one or more flagella, and cytoskeleton elements. **Eukaryotic cells** are generally larger than prokaryotic cells, contain linear, double-stranded DNA combined with histones and packaged as chromosomes. The chromosomes are found inside a nucleus bounded by two membranes. Eukaryotic cells contain a variety of other membrane-bound organelles such as mitochondria, chloroplasts, endoplasmic reticula, Golgi bodies, lysosomes, and vacuoles. Eukaryotic ribosomes are larger and more complex than those found in prokaryotes.

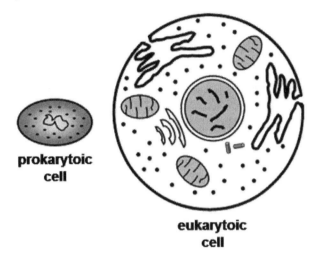

prokarytoic
cell

eukarytoic
cell

Food web in a freshwater system

In a typical freshwater food web, energy passes from autotrophs, or primary producers, through various levels of consumers. Energy passes to primary (small macroinvertebrates) and secondary consumers (small fishes, frogs, larger invertebrates) then moves through the web to tertiary consumers (larger fishes, herons, etc.). In turn, the autotrophs and consumers die and contribute to the organic matter and detritus found in the freshwater environment.

Gene synthesizing proteins

Genes are the hereditary units that code for specific proteins that determine how an organism looks and/or functions. When a specific protein is needed, the gene coding for that protein is "turned on" and its DNA segment is transcribed into a complementary strand of messenger RNA (mRNA). Ribosomes attach to the mRNA strand where they translate the mRNA sequence in order to build the specific protein. Specific versions of another type of RNA called transfer RNA (tRNA) are attached to specific amino acids. Codons formed of every three bases on the mRNA strand match up with anticodons on its intended tRNA to form a growing peptide chain of amino acids linked together by peptide bonds. This amino acid chain eventually becomes the peptide, or protein, coded for by that gene. In some viruses, genes are formed directly from RNA.

DNA_{gene} → mRNA → mRNA-ribosome complex + tRNA → growing peptide chain → protein

Mutation

A mutation is any change in the sequence of bases in a gene's DNA or RNA (in certain viruses). Such changes can be caused by ionizing radiation or mutagenic chemicals that cause base deletions or substitutions, viruses that inject their DNA into a host cell's genome, and errors that occur during DNA replication and/or meiosis (nondisjunction, recombination). These changes are inherited by the daughter cells during subsequent rounds of mitosis. Since mutations are random, most are harmful to the organism in some way, but a small percent are neutral or even advantageous. Neutral mutations do not have a negative or positive effect on an organism's survival, while advantageous ones enhance its chances of survival and reproduction. Thus, selectively advantageous mutations tend to accumulate in a population over time and lead to adaptations.

Photosynthesis

Photosynthesis is the process by which chlorophyll-containing autotrophs, such as plants, use the energy in sunlight to convert carbon dioxide and water into carbohydrates while releasing oxygen as a waste product. The reaction is light + 6 CO_2 + 12 H_2O --> $C_6H_{12}O_6$ + 6 O_2 + 6 H_2O. The process involves two stages, the light and dark reactions. In the light reaction, photons from light provide the energy to split a water molecule. The electrons released are boosted into higher energy states and generate reducing equivalents and the energy-carrying molecule, ATP. In the dark reaction, or Calvin-Benson cycle, atmospheric CO_2 is captured and converted by the reducing equivalents and ATP into 3-carbon sugars, and then later, converted into 6-carbon sugar phosphates and then into sucrose, starch, and cellulose.

Mitosis

Eukaryotic cells divide into two genetically identical daughter cells in a process called mitosis. Meiosis is another form of cell division that produces haploid gametes for sexual reproduction. At the beginning of mitosis, DNA chromatin condenses into chromosomes, which replicate themselves forming two sister chromatids joined by a centromere. These chromosomes line up along an equatorial plate in the center of the cell, the centromere divides, and each of the two paired chromatids is pulled to opposites sides of the cell by microtubules attached to the centromere and the star-shaped centrosome. The cytoplasm then divides in a process called cytokinesis. At the end of mitosis, the diploid ($2n$) genome of the original cell, the entirety of the parent cell's DNA, is passed on to each daughter cell.

Meiosis

Sexual reproduction in eukaryotic organisms involves a form of cell division known as meiosis, in which a diploid ($2n$) primary germ cell gives rise to haploid (n) gametes or spores. The diploid germ cell contains two exact copies of each chromosome (known as a homologous pair) in its genome, one from each parent. As in mitosis, meiosis begins by DNA replication and the doubling of each chromosome into two sister chromatids. The homologous pairs then come together along the equatorial plate and usually exchange fragments from one chromosome to the other—known as crossing over or recombination. Thus, genetic material from the paternal and maternal chromosomes are exchanged. The reshuffled homologous pairs are pulled to opposite poles of the cell and the cell divides to produce two $2n$ daughter cells that are genetically different from the parent cell (meiosis I). A second division (meiosis II) occurs next resulting in four haploid (n) gametes or spores. When two gametes combine during fertilization, a diploid zygote is formed.

Ccological succession

Ecological or seral succession is a basic concept in ecology. It refers to the generally predictable stages (seres) an ecological system undergoes before eventually arriving at a stable climax biotic community best adapted to the prevailing climate, soil, and other conditions in an area. Areas recently cleared of vegetation by fire, logging, volcanic eruptions or other disturbance are first colonized by pioneer organisms, such as grasses and herbaceous plants. After a few years, shrubs may appear followed by small, rapidly growing trees that require sunlight. As the trees mature, more and more shade-tolerant species appear until a climax community is attained. However, many biological communities undergo such rapid man-made or other disturbances that they cannot achieve their climax state. Nevertheless, the concept remains a valid description of old-growth or mature ecosystems, such as the northern boreal forest or taiga, the once widespread temperate deciduous forests of eastern North America, and the tropical rainforests of the world--all of which are fast disappearing due to logging and other human activities.

Extinction of the dinosaurs

Several factors appear to have jointly contributed to the Cretaceous-Tertiary (K-T) extinction event. Along with all non-avian dinosaurs, mosasaurs, pleisiosaurs and pterosaurs became extinct, as did many plants and marine invertebrates. However, mammals, birds, crocodilians, amphibians and many other major groups survived. The Deccan Traps in India indicate massive volcanic activity for the million years or so preceding the K-T event, which undoubtedly had major impacts on late Cretaceous biodiversity. The worldwide presence of a thin iridium layer at the K-T time period indicates that an asteroid impact occurred at that time with catastrophic results for the world's living organisms. The subsequent discovery of the Chixulub impact crater along the coast of Yucatán and its identification as the site of impact of the K-T asteroid proved the hypothesis. The demise of the dinosaurs probably began a million years earlier with the onset of the Deccan volcanism and was finished when the 10-kilometer wide asteroid hit Earth and altered conditions across the planet.

Carbon cycle

All organic life requires carbon as its base. Carbon dioxide (CO_2) is extracted primarily from the atmosphere and the oceans by plants and algae, respectively. Plants achieve this through photosynthesis, using energy from the sun to convert the atmospheric CO_2 into carbon-containing sugars. It is then absorbed in the bodies of the animals who consume the plants for food. The carbon continues to be passed up the food chain as the animals that ate the plants are consumed in turn by other animals. Carbon is continuously being released into the atmosphere in the form of CO_2 as a result of respiration. Animals that die without being consumed by other animals are broken down by decomposer organisms that eventually release the CO_2 back into the atmosphere. Plants are considered to be primary producers, since they take their carbon directly from the atmosphere, while organisms that obtain their carbon through consumption of other organisms are considered to be secondary producers.

Dichotomous key

A dichotomous key is tool that is frequently used to identify unknown or unfamiliar organisms in the natural world, such as trees, flowers, insects, mammals, reptiles, and fish. Dichotomous keys consist of a series of yes/no questions, usually asking about a single characteristic. Answering all of these questions accurately will lead to the accurate identification of the organism in question. The questions start with the features that allow for the broadest categorization and then gradually narrow down to the features identifying specific organisms. Below is a very simple example:

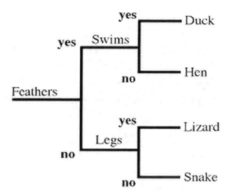

Examples

Example #1

A wooden block slides down a ramp inclined at 30 degrees. Attached to the back of the block is a string that threads through a pulley and lifts a smaller block, as shown in the diagram. List the forces acting on the wooden block and the direction of each force, and construct a free body force diagram for it. (Do not assume the ramp is frictionless.)

There are four forces acting on the wooden block: the force of gravity (weight), the normal force exerted on the block by the ramp, the tension on the string that pulls back on the block, and the force of kinetic friction. Gravity acts directly downward. The normal force is perpendicular to the surface of the ramp, and is therefore inclined 30 degrees from the vertical. Both the tension in the string and the force of kinetic friction act parallel to the ramp surface.

A sample free body diagram is shown here. Your free body diagram may be differently oriented, the vectors may be drawn with different apparent magnitudes, and the forces may be labeled with different symbols, but the relative directions of the forces should be as shown.

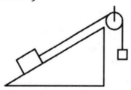

- 22 -

Example #2

A graph of a function is shown. Is it linear or nonlinear? When is the function increasing or decreasing?

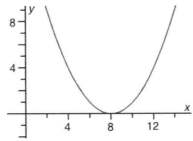

The function is nonlinear. If the function were linear, all of the points would fall in a straight line, resulting in a line graph. Any graph that is curved represents a nonlinear function. The function is increasing when the graph rises from left to right. Similarly, the function is decreasing when the graph falls from left to right. The graph appears to change from decreasing to increasing at the point (8, 0). This means that for $x < 8$, the function is decreasing. For $x > 8$, the function is increasing.

Example #3

Suppose a cart moves at constant acceleration along a track with a number of photogates spaced along it at known positions. Each photogate records the time at which the cart passes through it. From this data, explain how you would you determine the cart's average velocity over the entire track, its instantaneous velocity at a particular point on the track, and its acceleration.

The cart's average velocity is simply equal to its total displacement divided by the total time elapsed. In this case, the displacement is the distance between the first and last photogates, and the elapsed time is the difference between the times recorded by the first and last photogates.

True instantaneous velocity is impossible to measure directly with the equipment described here, but if two of the photogates are placed very close together, a good approximation can be found by taking the average velocity over a very small distance.

If we take two such approximations of the instantaneous velocity, the cart's acceleration can be (approximately) found by dividing the difference in the two velocities by the time elapsed between the two pairs of photogates.

Earth Sciences

Seasons of the Earth

Earth's rotational axis is tilted approximately 23.5° to its orbital axis around the Sun. Thus, depending on Earth's position in its revolution around the Sun, the northern and southern hemispheres are exposed to different amounts of direct sunlight from the Sun's rays. The Northern Hemisphere experiences summer, which means longer days and shorter nights when the North Pole is tilted toward the Sun. At the same time, the Southern Hemisphere is tilted away from the Sun and experiences the shorter days and longer nights of winter. The situation is reversed six months later when Earth has traveled to the opposite side of the Sun. The Northern Hemisphere experiences winter while the Southern Hemisphere is in summer. Because the shape of Earth's orbit around the Sun is an ellipse rather than a perfect circle, Earth is at aphelion (its farthest point from the Sun) during the northern summer/southern winter. Conversely, it is at perihelion (its closest point to the Sun) during the southern summer/northern winter.

Ocean tides on Earth

The main force behind ocean tides is the gravitational pull of the Moon on Earth's oceans. The Sun exerts a somewhat smaller influence. The rotation of Earth beneath the Moon's gravitational pull produces the twice daily tidal cycle. The tidal force is greatest on the ocean waters on the side nearest the Moon and smallest on the water on the side facing away from the Moon. Thus, a high tide, or bulge, results in the waters on the side facing the Moon because of the strong gravitational pull and another high tide occurs on the opposite side of Earth, furthest from the Moon because the water molecules on the far side are "left behind" and pile up.

Spring tides vs. neap tides

Ignoring the effects of elliptical orbits, the Sun exerts a tidal force approximately 46% of that of the Moon. When the Sun, Moon, and Earth are aligned at new moon and full moon phases, the tidal forces of the Sun and Moon reinforce each other to produce a maximum range between high and low tides. High tides are generally higher and low tides are lower than usual. These extreme tides are called **spring tides**. Conversely, when the Moon is in its first or third quarter phases, the positions of the Sun, Earth, and Moon form a right angle and the tidal pull of the Sun and Moon reduce each other's effect. There is much less difference between high tides and low tides during this period. These minimal tidal ranges are called **neap tides**.

Bodies of the solar system

Our solar system consists of the Sun, a G-class star, around which eight major planets orbit. In order of their distance from the Sun, the planets are Mercury, Venus, Earth, Mars, Jupiter, Saturn, Uranus, and Neptune. The first four planets are the inner planets, which are small with solid, rocky surfaces. The four outer planets are the gas giants. They are very large and made up almost entirely of gas with no solid surfaces. Between Mars and Jupiter lies an asteroid belt of small, rocky objects of varying size. Pluto, once considered the ninth planet, has been downgraded from planetary status and is now called a dwarf planet, like many other similar-sized objects beyond Neptune's orbit. Five of these objects, including Pluto, are large enough to gravitationally form spheres and are regarded as minor planets. The Kuiper Belt extends beyond Neptune from 30 astronomical units (AU) to about 50 AU. One AU is the mean distance from the Sun to Earth, approximately 150 million kilometers. The Kuiper Belt contains countless numbers of icy bodies of water, methane, and ammonia, some with rocky cores. Beyond the Kuiper Belt is the spherical Oort Cloud, thought to be the source of long-period comets. It lies at a distance of about 1 light-year (~9.5 trillion km) from the Sun.

Milky Way galaxy

The Milky Way galaxy is a giant spiral galaxy some 100,000 light-years (ly), or about 9.46×10^{17} kilometers (~946 thousand trillion km) in diameter. Recent evidence suggests that the Milky Way has a central bar and may have to be reclassified as a "barred spiral" or intermediate type galaxy. It contains about 200 billion stars and is one of at least 200 billion galaxies in the known Universe. It is home to our Sun and its solar system, located about 26,000 light-years (~246 thousand trillion km, or a little over halfway out) from the galactic center on the inner edge of the Orion-Cygnus arm. Like the galaxy's size, the exact distance is not precisely known because of clouds of gas and dust that obscure our view from Earth. Our solar system revolves around the center of the galaxy approximately once every 250 million years.

Stars, red giants, and white dwarfs

The Sun is a main-sequence star, about 1.4 million kilometers in diameter. Betelgeuse is a red supergiant, approximately 825 million kilometers in diameter located 640 light-years from the Sun. If Betelgeuse were located at the Sun's position, it would extend past the orbit of Jupiter. In a scale model, if the Sun were the size of a dime (1.8 cm in diameter), the diameter of Betelgeuse would be just 3 meters less than the length of a regulation NFL football field, including both end zones (107.6 m). On the other hand, a white dwarf would be about the size of a small bacterium (1.6 μm) and a red dwarf would be about half the size of a sesame seed (about 1.5 mm). The largest known star, the hypergiant VY Canis Majoris, is over 3 billion kilometers in diameter and is located 4,900 light-years from Earth. Most red giants are considerably smaller than Betelgeuse or VY Canis Majoris, but are still 25–50 times the diameter of the Sun.

Plate tectonics

Earth's crust is made up of a dozen or so major lithospheric (crustal) plates that float upon Earth's mantle (aesthenosphere). These plates move about each other in response to complex convection currents set in motion by Earth's interior heat. Two plates move apart from each other at divergent boundaries, or spreading centers, and come together at convergent boundaries. Left and right lateral strike-slip movement between plates occurs along transform faults often resulting in an earthquake. Where thin, dense, mafic (iron and magnesium rich) oceanic crust collides with thick, light, sialic (silica rich) continental crust, the oceanic crust subducts beneath the continental crust. The subducted material carries scraped off continental crust and seawater down with it. As this material melts, it rises as a mixture of magma and steam to produce explosive volcanic mountain ranges like those ringing the Pacific Ocean Basin. On the other hand, when two continental plates collide at convergent boundaries, the crust buckles thrusting up massive mountain ranges like the Alps and Himalayas.

Earthquakes

Causes of earthquakes

Earthquakes happen when energy is suddenly released causing a movement of the ground. This can be due to sudden slippage along faults, crustal plate boundaries, or at mid-oceanic seafloor spreading zones. When accumulated stress (potential energy) from plate tectonic movement is suddenly released as kinetic energy, the ground shifts and an earthquake occurs. A combination of

- 25 -

upwelling convection currents in the mantle at seafloor spreading zones and tensile forces pulling the plates apart under their own weight at subduction zones cause oceanic plates to move past one another. The rate of movement can vary from 2.5 cm per year at the Mid-Atlantic Ridge to 13 cm per year along the East Pacific Rise. This movement causes stresses along faults and other zones of lithospheric weakness. Large sections of crust become locked in place because of friction as the stresses accumulate. When the stress builds up enough to overcome the friction, a sudden slippage occurs, generating earthquakes. Earthquakes can also be caused by volcanic activity, massive landslides, nuclear explosions, and other events.

Measuring earthquake intensity

Earthquakes are commonly measured with seismometers, which convert wave energy into a magnitude on a logarithmic scale. The magnitude of earthquakes is measured on a scale commonly referred to as the "Richter scale". However, large earthquakes (8 and higher) maximize at about 7 on the older, outdated Richter scale, which is best used for local quakes measuring 5 or less. Large quakes are measured worldwide on the moment magnitude (M_W) scale, which takes the total energy released into account. The M_W and Richter scales coincide over the medium range of earthquake intensities, but diverge at small and large intensities. An increase of one unit on the Richter or moment magnitude scales equals 10 times the amount of shaking and a $10^{1.5}$ (31.6-fold) increase in released energy. An increase of two units equals an increase in amplitude and energy of 100 and 1000 times, respectively. For example, an earthquake of magnitude 6 on the Richter scale is 100 times "stronger" than a magnitude 4 earthquake. Other seismograph-based "Richter" scales include the body-wave and surface-wave magnitude scales.

Tornado

A tornado is a violent rotating column of air usually extending from a severe thunderstorm to contact Earth's surface on either land or water. Tornadoes can occur almost anywhere in the world (except Antarctica), but the most common and dangerous ones occur in the United States between the Rocky Mountains and Appalachian Mountains in an area nicknamed "Tornado Alley". The rotating column of air is invisible until a funnel forms from condensed water droplets and/or dust and debris from the ground. The extreme rotating wind speeds reduce pressure inside the funnel significantly (Bernoulli's principle). The expanding air molecules inside this low-pressure vortex perform work causing the temperature to drop until water vapor condenses into visible droplets, forming a condensation funnel. An F0 tornado on the Fujita scale has wind speeds of 64–116 km/h (40–72 mph) and cause minimal damage. The most violent F5 tornados can have wind speeds over 500 km/h (310 mph) and cause catastrophic damage and loss of life. Fortunately, F5 tornadoes are rare.

Rotation of low pressure systems in the Northern Hemisphere

In a rotating reference frame, such as the Earth rotating on its axis, inertial motion is deflected to the right when the rotation is counterclockwise like the Northern Hemisphere when viewed from the North Pole. This is due to the Coriolis effect, a fictitious "force" arising from a rotating reference frame. In a low pressure system, there is less air present than normal. This causes nearby air to rush in and fill the space. As the air rushes in, it is deflected to the right, in the Northern Hemisphere. As the air veers right, it is pushed by other air masses that are also trying to move toward the center of the low pressure area. This causes all the air to spin in a circle counter-clockwise. The opposite is true in the Southern Hemisphere—the system rotates clockwise.

- 26 -

El Niño-Southern Oscillation (ENSO) event

Normally, the westerly trade winds push the tropical coastal surface water along the Pacific coast of Ecuador and Peru offshore toward the western Pacific Ocean. This displaced surface water is replaced by cold, nutrient-rich water that rises from lower ocean depths. The deep water supports rich phytoplankton growth and healthy fish stocks. The equatorial western Pacific is also normally dominated by warm, humid, low-pressure winds. This helps with the westward movement of surface water. ENSO events are randomly triggered every few years when atmospheric pressure increases in the western Pacific and Indian Ocean while decreasing in the central and eastern Pacific. It is also supported by trade winds that diminish or even reverse. During an *El Niño* event, less surface water is displaced westward causing less cold, nutrient-rich water to rise from below. This results in catastrophic economic losses to the local fisheries and causes major impacts on worldwide weather including droughts and floods. *El Niño* literally translates to "the boy" in Spanish and it refers to the Christ Child because the phenomenon usually occurs around Christmas. Strong ENSO events are often followed by opposite conditions known as *La Nina*.

Climate vs. weather

Climate refers to the typical patterns of temperature, humidity, type and amount of precipitation, winds, seasonal patterns, and other atmospheric and meteorological phenomena of a region over many years. Climate is influenced by both latitude and longitude, altitude, geography, and proximity to mountain ranges or large bodies of water. Climate can also apply to the planet as a whole when referring to epochs, such as Ice Ages. In contrast, weather is the short-term day-to-day variation in meteorological conditions of a given region. Weather is what is reported on the news each day. An example comparing the two is that the climate of Southern California is dry and sunny, but the weather on Tuesday will be rainy.

Mountain temperature vs. valley/plain temperature

Temperature is related to altitude and since mountains have greater altitude than valleys or plains, they are cooler. As altitude increases, there is less atmosphere pressing down upon the surface. When the pressure on a gas is reduced it expands and cools without exchanging any heat with the surrounding air mass. As the gas molecules expand, they exert work against the surrounding atmosphere to push it aside. In doing so, they lose kinetic energy causing the temperature to drop. Conversely, increased pressure exerts work against the gas molecules, causing them to gain kinetic energy (move faster) and heat up. For example, a tire gets warmer as you pump air into it.

Igneous, sedimentary, and metamorphic rocks

Igneous rock forms when hot magma or lava cools beneath or above the ground, respectively, to form large- or fine-grained crystalline, porous, or glassy rocks of varying chemical composition. Sedimentary rocks form from previously weathered and eroded material, which may have been igneous, sedimentary, or metamorphic rock. This weathered material deposits out in layers and eventually becomes compacted and/or chemically solidified into rock. Sedimentary rocks, like limestone and dolomite, can also form from the compaction of calcium carbonate exoskeletons of aquatic organisms. Sediments can also form from the precipitation of salts from evaporating bodies of water. Metamorphic rocks are altered, partially re-melted, and generally highly crystalline igneous, sedimentary, or even older metamorphic rocks that have undergone extreme amounts of heat and compression. Anthracite coal is a highly metamorphosed coal. Volcanic sills and dikes can produce contact metamorphism in immediately adjacent rock, while uplifting mountain ranges result in large-scale regional metamorphism.

Hertzsprung-Russell diagram

The Hertzsprung-Russell (H-R) diagram shows stars at various stages of their evolution according to their luminosity (or absolute magnitude) and surface temperature in kelvins (K). Luminosity is the amount of energy a star radiates per second ($L_\odot$) and is usually compared to our Sun. Most stars lie along a band called the main sequence, ranging from very large, hot, bright giant stars at upper left to smaller, cooler red dwarfs at lower right. The Sun, lies right in the middle of the diagram. Stars like the Sun occupy the main sequence for 10 billion years or so before using up all of the hydrogen fuel in their cores. Hydrogen (nuclear) fusion then moves out from the core and the star swells into a red giant near the end of its life. Stars like the Sun will eventually shed much of their mass as a planetary nebula and collapse into white dwarfs. The most massive stars die in a violent explosion called a supernova; the remaining mass collapses into a neutron star or a black hole.

Measures of distance used in astronomy

Various measures are used for astronomical distances. The distance known as a **light-year** (ly) is equal to the distance that light can travel in one year. Light travels at about 300,000,000 m/s in a vacuum. In a year, light will travel about 9.45 trillion kilometers. The Sun at 150 million km from Earth is about 8⅓ light-*minutes* away. The nearest star to the Sun, Proxima Centauri, is 4.2 ly away. Another distance measurement, the **astronomical unit (**AU), is the mean distance from the Sun to Earth: 1 AU = ~150 million km. The mean distance from the Sun to Neptune is about 30 AU. The **parsec** (pc), another unit for measuring large distances, is defined as the distance from the Sun which would produce a parallax of 1 arc-second as seen from Earth's revolution around the Sun. The distance can be calculated using simple trigonometry; 1 pc = 3.26 ly. For truly large distances kiloparsecs (10^3 pc, or kpc) and megaparsecs (10^6 pc, or Mpc) are used.

Determining the distance to a nearby star

Astronomers use parallax, shown in the geometry of the diagram below, and trigonometry and to calculate astronomical distances.

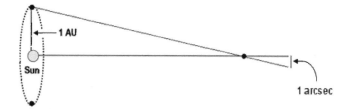

Solar system

The **solar sy**stem consists of the sun and eight **major planets**. In order from the sun the planets are Mercury, Venus, Earth, Mars, Jupiter, Saturn, Uranus and Neptune. Pluto is no longer considered to be a major planet. Along with 5 other similar sized objects it is now a **minor pla**net. Six of the major planets have one or more moons. The solar system also contains countless **meteoroids**, **asteroid**s, and **comet**s.

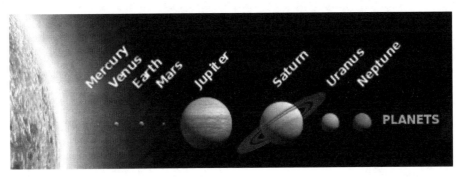

Galaxies

Galaxies consist of stars, stellar remnants, and dark matter. Dwarf galaxies contain as few as 10 million stars, while giant galaxies contain as many as 1 trillion stars. Galaxies are gravitationally bound, meaning the stars, star systems, other gases, and dust orbits the galaxy's center. The Earth exists in the Milky Way galaxy and the nearest galaxy to ours is the Andromeda galaxy. Galaxies can be classified by their visual shape into elliptical, spiral, irregular, and starburst galaxies. It is estimated that there are more than 100 billion galaxies in the universe ranging from 1,000 to 100,000 parsecs in diameter. Galaxies can be megaparsecs apart. Intergalactic space consists of a gas with an average density of less than one atom per cubic meter. Galaxies are organized into clusters which form superclusters. Dark matter may account for up to 90% of the mass of galaxies. Dark matter is still not well understood.

Astronomical unit, light year, and parsec

An astronomical unit, also known as AU, is a widely used measurement in astronomy. One AU is equal to the distance from the Earth to the Sun, which is 150 million km, or 93 million miles. These distances can also be expressed as 149.60×10^9 m or 92.956×10^6 mi. A light year (ly) is the distance that light travels in a vacuum in one year. A light year is equal to about 10 trillion km, or 64,341 AU, and is used to measure large astronomical units. Also used for measuring large distances is the parsec (pc), which is the preferred unit since it is better suited for recording observational data. A parsec is the parallax of one arcsecond, and is about 31 trillion km (about 19 trillion miles), or about 3.26 light years. It is used to calculate distances by triangulation. The AU distance from the Earth to the Sun is used to form the side of a right triangle.

Formation of the solar system theories

A planetary system consists of the various non-stellar objects orbiting a star, such as planets, dwarf planets, moons, asteroids, meteoroids, comets, and cosmic dust. The Sun, together with its planetary system, which includes Earth, is known as the solar system. The theory of how the solar system was created is that it started with the collapse of a cloud of interstellar gas and dust, which formed the solar nebula. This collapse is believed to have occurred because the cloud was disturbed. As it collapsed, it heated up and compressed at the center, forming a flatter protoplanetary disk with a protostar at the center. Planets formed as a result of accretion from the disk. Gas cooled and condensed into tiny particles of rock, metal, and ice. These particles collided and formed into larger particles, and then into object the size of small asteroids. Eventually, some became large enough to have significant gravity.

Topographic maps and satellite views

A topographic map is a type of map that gives details about the surface of the earth in a given area, primarily depicting features such as elevation changes and bodies of water, both natural and man-made. They are frequently published in sets, where several smaller maps can be pieced together to represent a large area. Topographic maps represent elevation by using contour lines to indicate the areas on the map that have a particular exact elevation. A hill or mountain being depicted on a topographic map will have multiple contour lines encircling it. Topographic maps are used for a variety of applications in industries such as construction and mining, and recreationally for sports such as hiking and orienteering.

A satellite view is the view of a region from the perspective of someone looking down from high above the earth. These images are frequently taken from satellites orbiting the earth, but many of the images referred to as satellite views are taken from aircraft flying inside the atmosphere. Satellite-view images are commonly used to see the details of land formations, erosion features, and weather conditions.

Gravity

Gravity is the universal force that causes large objects to attract other nearby objects. The sun is the largest body in our solar system and it attracts all other bodies toward itself. This gravitational pull is what keeps all of the planets in orbit around the sun. The pull that the sun exerts is proportional to the size of the object it is attracting and its distance from the object. Small objects such as those we encounter in our daily lives on the earth also exert a proportionately-sized pull on other objects, but the effect is not measurable when observed so close to the gravitational pull of the earth.

Investigation And Experimentation

Physical changes

Physical changes are those that do not affect the chemical properties of a substance. Changes in state are physical changes. For example, a liquid can freeze into a solid or boil into a gas, but its chemical nature remains the same. Ice, steam, and liquid water are all still water (H_2O). Physical properties include features such as shape, texture, size, color, odor, volume, mass, and density, although some changes in color or odor can indicate chemical changes. Certain changes such as the dissolution of ionic or polar compounds in a solvent are considered physical changes even though they involve breaking chemical bonds. If a saltwater solution evaporates, crystalline table salt will be left behind as a precipitate; adding water will produce a new saltwater solution.

Materials denser than water

Ships and other floating objects made of materials that are denser than water float because of the empty space they contain inside their hulls. A ship weighing 5,000 tons overall will displace 5,000 tons of water, but this weight of water will occupy a smaller volume than the ship itself. Once this amount of water has been displaced the ship will not sink any deeper into the water and will float. Archimedes' principle states that the buoyant force is equal to the weight of the water (or any other fluid displaced). The reason a solid piece of iron or a rock sinks is that it weighs more than the volume of water it displaces. For the same reason, because a helium-filled balloon is lighter than air it will rise until the air's density is reduced such that the volume of air displaced is the same as the volume of the balloon.

Three domains of living organisms

Domain Bacteria	Domain *Archaea*	Domain *Eukarya*
prokaryotic grade	prokaryotic grade	eukaryotic grade
Division	Division	Kingdom
Proteobacteria	Euryarchaeota	Protista
Division	Division	Kingdom
Cyanobacteria	Crenarchaeota	Fungi
Division	Division	Kingdom
Gram-positive bacteria	Korarchaeota	Plantae
Division	Nanoarchaeota	Kingdom
Chlamydiae		Animalia

Scientific hypotheses vs. theories

A scientific **hypothesis** is a falsifiable (testable), plausible, proposed explanation for a natural phenomenon or set of observations that is consistent with the known body of scientific information. A good hypothesis leads to one or more predictions (if *this* is true, then *that* should follow) which can be tested by further observations or experimentation. If the predictions are supported by the evidence of the test(s) it becomes provisionally accepted as a working hypothesis subject to further research and testing. If the hypothesis is not supported by the test(s), it must be rejected and a new explanation sought. One or more of equally plausible competing hypotheses may be favored because of testability (falsifiability), simplicity (adherence to the principle of parsimony in requiring the fewest assumptions), and scope (applicability to the widest range of phenomena). A scientific **theory** is an exhaustively tested and greatly expanded hypothesis that explains a vast array of scientific phenomena and observations and neatly complements and augments all other scientific theories and observations. It is as close to a factual explanation as science can achieve.

Periodic table

The periodic table groups elements with similar chemical properties together. The grouping of elements is based on atomic structure. It shows periodic trends of physical and chemical properties and identifies families of elements with similar properties. It is a common model for organizing and understanding elements. In the periodic table, each element has its own cell that includes varying amounts of information presented in symbol form about the properties of the element. Cells in the table are arranged in rows (periods) and columns (groups or families). At minimum, a cell includes the symbol for the element and its atomic number. The cell for hydrogen, for example, which appears first in the upper left corner, includes an "H" and a "1" above the letter. Elements are ordered by atomic number, left to right, top to bottom.

Significance of groups and periods in the periodic table

A group is a vertical column of the periodic table. Elements in the same group have the same number of valence electrons. For the representative elements, the number of valence electrons is equal to the group number. Because of their equal valence electrons, elements in the same groups have similar physical and chemical properties. A period is a horizontal row of the periodic table. Atomic number increases from left to right across a row. The period of an element corresponds to the highest energy level of the electrons in the atoms of that element. The energy level increases from top to bottom down a group.

Periodic table groups

In the periodic table, the groups are the columns numbered 1 through 18 that group elements with similar outer electron shell configurations. Previous naming conventions for groups have included the use of Roman numerals and upper-case letters. Currently, the periodic table groups are: Group 1, alkali metals or lithium family; Group 2, alkaline earth metals or beryllium family; Group 3, scandium family; Group 4, titanium family; Group 5, vanadium family; Group 6, chromium family; Group 7, manganese family; Group 8, iron family; Group 9, cobalt family; Group 10, nickel family; Group 11, coinage metals or copper family; Group 12, zinc family; Group 13, boron family; Group 14; carbon family; Group 15, pnictogens or nitrogen family; Group 16, chalcogens or oxygen family; Group 17, halogens or fluorine family; Group 18, helium family and neon family (includes the first six periods, which are the noble gases).

Arrangement of metals, nonmetals, and metalloids

The metals are located on the left side and center of the periodic table, and the nonmetals are located on the right side of the periodic table. The metalloids or semimetals form a zigzag line between the metals and nonmetals as shown below. Metals include the alkali metals such as lithium, sodium, and potassium and the alkaline earth metals such as beryllium, magnesium, and calcium. Metals also include the transition metals such as iron, copper, and nickel and the inner transition metals such as thorium, uranium, and plutonium. Nonmetals include the chalcogens such as oxygen and sulfur, the halogens such as fluorine and chlorine, and the noble gases such as helium

- 32 -

and argon. Carbon, nitrogen, and phosphorus are also nonmetals. Metalloids or semimetals include boron, silicon, germanium, antimony, and polonium.

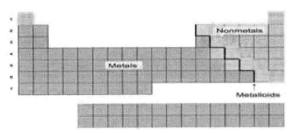

Chemical families on the periodic table

Chemical families of elements are groups of elements with very similar chemical properties. These families are grouped together on the periodic table. Several of these families have elements that fall in a single column on the table. Note: In this context, oxidation number can be viewed as the charge of the ion formed by the element.

1. alkali metals—Group 1 (1A): These elements are contained in the first column of the periodic table, and the oxidation number of each is 1+. These elements are extremely reactive; they react violently with water.
2. alkaline earth metals—Group 2 (2A): The alkaline earth metals are in the second column of the periodic table. All elements in this group have an oxidation number of 2+. They are very reactive but not as much as the alkali metals.
3. halogens—Group 17 (7A): The halogens are in the second column from the right on the periodic table. The oxidation number of these elements is 1-. They are the most reactive of the nonmetals.
4. noble gases—Group 18 (8A): The noble gases are in the last column of the periodic table. The oxidation number of these elements is generally given as 0, although there are some exceptions. These elements do not tend to react chemically with any substances.

Atomic radii on the periodic table

Moving from left to right across the periodic table, the atomic radius decreases as the atomic number increases. At first glance, this may seem contrary to what you would expect. As the number of protons in the nucleus increases, the overall positive charge of the nucleus increases. This means that the strength with which the nucleus attracts the electrons increases, causing them to be pulled in more closely to the nucleus.

Atomic radii increase moving down in the periodic table. The elements in each period of the periodic table have outer electrons that in a higher energy level than the period above it. These outer electrons' shells are partially shielded from the attractive force of the nucleus by the inner shells. This weakens the attractive force and allows the outer electrons to move farther away from the nucleus.

Trends of physical properties of the elements

The boiling point, melting point, and conductivity of the elements depend partially on the number of valence electrons of the atoms of those elements. For the representative elements in groups 1A–8A, the number of valence electrons matches the group number. Because all of the elements in each individual group contain the same number of valence electrons, elements in the same groups tend to have similar boiling points, melting points, and conductivity. Boiling points and melting points tend to decrease moving down the column of groups 1A–4A and 8A but increase slightly moving down the column of groups 5A–7A.

Net force acting on an object

The net force is the sum of all the forces acting on an object. Since force is a vector, the net force is a vector sum; simply adding together the magnitudes of all the forces will not yield the correct net force. To determine the net force, the components along the x- and y-axis of each force acting on the object must be determined, and these x-components and y-components must be separately summed to obtain the x- and y- components of the net force; the magnitude of the net force can be calculated from these components. (Alternately, the net force can be determined graphically by drawing the vectors representing the individual forces end-to-end, but this method is generally less accurate.)

The net force is important because it determines the motion of an object; the individual forces acting on the object do not, as forces in different directions may wholly or partially cancel each other out.

Free body force diagrams

A free body force diagram is a pictorial representation of the forces acting upon an object, and their directions. It is useful to help see how the forces on an object might interact, and how the components of each force combine when calculating the net force on the object (or calculating the magnitude and direction of an unknown force if the net force is known). Two perpendicular directions are chosen and, referring to the free body diagram, the components of the forces in each of those directions are added together to get the corresponding component of the net force.

To construct a free body diagram, first draw a symbol representing the object, fix one point as the center of mass, and then draw a force vector, an arrow from the center of mass, representing each force. The arrows should be drawn in the same directions as the corresponding forces. Optionally, they can also be drawn with lengths proportional to the forces' magnitudes.

States of matter

The three states of matter are **solids**, **liquids**, and **gases**. In a solid the **atoms** or **molecules** of a substance are close together and locked into place. The solid has a definite shape and volume. In a liquid the atoms or molecules are farther apart. A liquid flows and takes the shape of its container. In a gas the atoms or molecules are very far apart and have a lot of energy. They will fly completely way if not held inside a container like a balloon or a closed bottle.

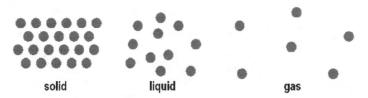

solid   liquid   gas

Comet

Comets are small icy bodies ranging in size from tens of yards to tens of miles in diameter. They orbit the sun with periods of a few years to hundreds of thousands of years. Halley's comet shown here orbits the sun every 75 to 76 years. As a comet nears the sun a long tail or coma is created as

- 34 -

ice and dust are blown off by the intense radiation and the solar wind of charged particles from the sun.

Meteoroids and meteors

A **meteoroid** is a sand- to boulder-sized piece of debris hurtling through the solar system at speeds of between 15 and 45 miles per second. When it enters earth's atmosphere it burns up and leaves a visible fiery trail of gas and debris called a **meteor**. Some meteoroids are large enough that they do not completely burn up, and what remains reaches the ground. These are called **meteorites**. Meteoroids can be small pieces that have broken off of **asteroids**.

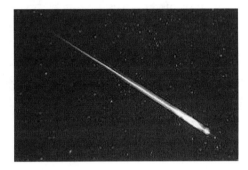

Function vs. structure of cells in living organisms

The functions of plant and animal cells vary greatly, and the functions of different cells within a single organism can also be vastly different. Animal and plant cells are similar in structure in that they are eukaryotic, which means they contain a nucleus. The nucleus is a round structure that controls the activities of the cell and contains chromosomes. Both types of cells have cell membranes, cytoplasm, vacuoles, and other structures. The main difference between the two is that plant cells have a cell wall made of cellulose that can handle high levels of pressure within the cell, which can occur when liquid enters a plant cell. Plant cells have chloroplasts that are used during the process of photosynthesis, which is the conversion of sunlight into food. Plant cells usually have one large vacuole, whereas animal cells can have many smaller ones. Plant cells have a regular shape, while the shapes of animal cells can vary.

Atomic number, neutrons, nucleon, and element

- Atomic number (proton number): The atomic number of an element refers to the number of protons in the nucleus of an atom. It is a unique identifier. It can be represented as Z. Atoms with a neutral charge have an atomic number that is equal to the number of electrons.
- Neutrons: Neutrons are the uncharged atomic particles contained within the nucleus. The number of neutrons in a nucleus can be represented as "N."
- Nucleon: This refers collectively to the neutrons and protons.

- Element: An element is matter with one particular type of atom. It can be identified by its atomic number, or the number of protons in its nucleus. There are approximately 117 elements currently known, 94 of which occur naturally on Earth. Elements from the periodic table include hydrogen, carbon, iron, helium, mercury, and oxygen.

Importance of forming a hypothesis

It is important to form a hypothesis in order to make a tentative explanation that accounts for an unbiased observation. To be scientific, the hypothesis must be testable through experimentation. Careful construction of the experiment provides that predictions derived from the hypothesis are valid. The hypothesis must be formulated in a manner designed to provide a framework for evaluating the results of an experiment. In many scientific experiments, a hypothesis is posited in negative terms because scientists may accept logically plausible ideas until they are proven false. It is more difficult to prove that a hypothesis is true because its validity must be proven in all possible situations under endless variable conditions. Scientists tend to construct hypotheses for testing by creating experiments that might prove them false. If they succeed, the hypothesis must be modified or discarded.

A hypothesis is a prediction of the outcome of the scientific investigation. In order to form a reasonable hypothesis, a significant amount of observation must first be accomplished followed by a valid problem being stated. A good hypothesis should be a prediction, and it must be testable. A good hypothesis should take into account the available background information on the topic, and it must be able to be proven wrong by a valid test. In chemistry, a valid test of a good hypothesis will typically consist of a controlled experiment that has only one variable and several constants. The test should either prove or disprove the hypothesis.

Average velocity

There are two types of velocity that are commonly considered in physics: average velocity and instantaneous velocity. If we want to calculate the *average velocity* of an object, we must know two things. First, we must know its displacement, or the distance it has covered. Second, we must know the time it took to cover this distance. Once we have this information, the formula for average velocity is quite simple: $v_{av} = (x_f - x_i)/(t_f - t_i)$, where the subscripts i and f denote the intial and final values of the position and time. In other words, the average velocity is equal to the change in position divided by the change in time. This calculation will indicate the average distance that was covered per unit of time. Average velocity is a vector and will always point in the same direction as the displacement vector (since time is a scalar and always positive).

Archimedes' principle

If an object is submerged in water, it will have a buoyant force exerted on it in the upward direction. This force is caused by the water pressure acting on the bottom surface of the object. The deeper the object is submerged, the greater the pressure at the bottom surface. Often, of course, this buoyant force is much too small to keep an object from sinking to the bottom. This idea of buoyancy is summarized in Archimedes' principle: a body wholly or partially submerged in a fluid will be buoyed up by a force equal to the weight of the fluid displaced by the body. Thus, an object's ability to remain afloat in a fluid depends on its density relative to that of the fluid. If the fluid has a higher density than the object, it will float. Otherwise, it will sink. This principle can also be used to find the weight of a floating object by calculating the volume of fluid that it has displaced. For instance if a cube with a volume of 1 m³ is floating in water to a depth of 0.25 m, the cube is

- 36 -

displacing 0.25 m³ of water. This is the equivalent of 250 kg of water, creating a buoyancy force of 2450 N. Thus, the block weighs 2450 N, has a mass of 250 kg, and has a density of 250 kg/m³.

Conservation of mass number and charge in nuclear reactions

Mass number is the sum of neutrons and protons in the nucleus ($A = N + Z$). The conservation of mass number is a concept related to nuclear reactions. Two conditions are required to balance a nuclear reaction. They are conservation of mass number and conservation of nuclear charge. In a nuclear equation, the mass numbers should be equal on each side of the arrow. In this type of equation, the mass number is in superscript in front of the element and the atomic number is in subscript. The total number of nucleons is the same even though the product elements are different. For example, when a specific isotope of uranium decays into thorium and helium, the original mass number of uranium is 238. After the reaction, the mass number of thorium is 234 and the mass number of helium is 4 ($238 = 234 + 4$). The mass number is the same on both sides of the equation.

Chemical vs. physical changes

Physical changes do not produce new substances. The atoms or molecules may be rearranged, but no new substances are formed. Phase changes or changes of state such as melting, freezing, and sublimation are physical changes. For example, physical changes include the melting of ice, the boiling of water, sugar dissolving into water, and the crushing of a piece of chalk into a fine powder. Chemical changes involve a chemical reaction and do produce new substances. When iron rusts, iron oxide is formed, indicating a chemical change. Other examples of chemical changes include baking a cake, burning wood, digesting a cracker, and mixing an acid and a base.

Change in enthalpy in chemical/physical processes

All chemical processes involve either the release or the absorption of heat. Enthalpy is this heat energy. Enthalpy is a state function that is equivalent to the amount of heat a system exchanges with its surroundings. For exothermic processes, which release heat, the change in enthalpy (ΔH) is negative because the final enthalpy is less than the initial enthalpy. For endothermic processes, which absorb heat, the change in enthalpy (ΔH) is positive because the final enthalpy is greater than the initial enthalpy.

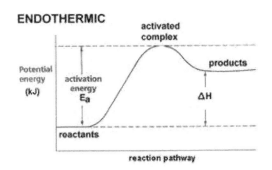 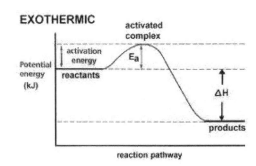

Carbon cycle

The carbon cycle is a biogeochemical cycle that describes the continuous movement of the Earth's carbon. Carbon is in the atmosphere, the soil, living organisms, fossil fuels, oceans, and freshwater systems. These areas are referred to as carbon reservoirs. Carbon flows between these reservoirs in an exchange called the carbon cycle. In the atmosphere, carbon is in the form of carbon dioxide. Carbon moves from the atmosphere to plants through the process of photosynthesis. Carbon moves from plants to animals through food chains. Carbon moves from living organisms to the soil when these organisms die. Carbon moves from living organisms to the atmosphere through cellular respiration. Carbon moves from fossil fuels to the atmosphere when fossil fuels are burned. Carbon moves from the atmosphere to the oceans and freshwater systems through absorption.

The carbon cycle

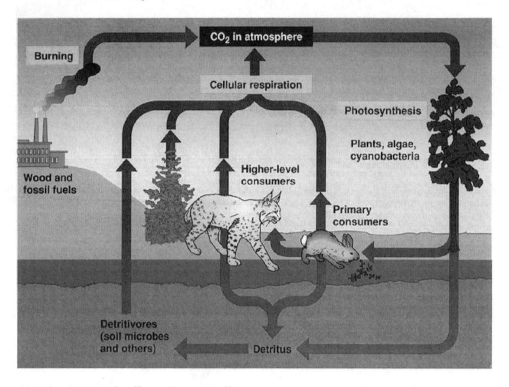

Structure and function of cells and organelles

Plant cells and animal cells both have a nucleus, cytoplasm, cell membrane, ribosomes, mitochondria, endoplasmic reticulum, Golgi apparatus, and vacuoles. Plant cells have only one or two extremely large vacuoles. Animal cells typically have several small vacuoles. Plant cells have chloroplasts for photosynthesis because plants are autotrophs. Animal cells do not have chloroplasts because they are heterotrophs. Plant cells have a rectangular shape due to the cell wall,

- 38 -

and animal cells have more of a circular shape. Animal cells have centrioles, but only some plant cells have centrioles.

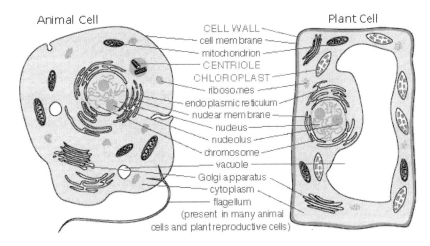

Oort Cloud, the asteroid belt, and the Kuiper Belt

The asteroid belt is between Mars and Jupiter. The many objects contained within are composed of rock and metal similar to those found on the terrestrial planets. The Kuiper Belt is beyond Neptune's orbit, but the influence of the gas giants may cause objects from the Kuiper Belt to cross Neptune's orbit. Objects in the Kuiper Belt are still being discovered. They are thought to be composed of the frozen forms of water, ammonia, and methane, and may be the source of short-period comets. It is estimated that there are 35,000 Kuiper Belt objects greater than 100 km in diameter and perhaps 100 million objects about 20 km in diameter. There is also a hypothetical Oort Cloud that may exist far beyond the Kuiper Belt and act as a source for long-period comets.

Practice Test #1

Practice Questions

1. Weather forecasters will sometimes use the phrase "the mercury will rise" for a forecasted hot day. Why does mercury rise?

    a. Molecules within the thermometer expand because of the hotter temperature. As they expand, they move up the thermometer.
    b. The neck of the thermometer becomes skinnier, making the mercury rise.
    c. Molecules within the thermometer shrink as the temperature gets hotter, and as they do so, move up the thermometer.
    d. The phrase has nothing to do with the outside temperature.

2. While in class, the teacher states that students will be working with a substance that is potentially combustible. Which of the following is not needed to work with this substance?

    a. Safety goggles
    b. Knowing the location of the fire extinguisher
    c. Lab coat
    d. Rubber boots

3. A student notices that every Monday the class has a quiz and that many of the students are not prepared. They begin to record the teacher's pattern of giving quizzes and notice that the quizzes fall on a Monday and cover the taught two weeks prior. What have the students noticed?

    a. An observation
    b. A trial
    c. A trend
    d. A model

Questions 4–5 pertain to the following chart:

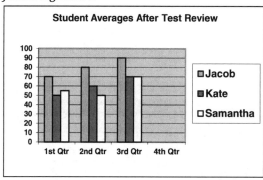

4. Using the table above, which student is likely to receive a 100% for the fourth quarter should this trend continue?

    a. Jacob
    b. Kate
    c. Samantha
    d. None of them

5. Using the table above, what conclusions can be made about the students' scores?

    a. The scores increased as the year progressed
    b. The girls did better than the boys on the test each quarter
    c. The test was about Math
    d. The scores were heavily impacted by the test reviews that were provided

6. In your garden, you noticed that the tomato plants did better on the North side of your house than the West side and you decided to figure out why. They are both planted with the same soil that provides adequate nutrients to the plant, and they are watered at the same time during the week. Over the course of a week, you begin to measure the amount of sunlight that hits each side of the house and determine that the North side gets more light because the sunlight is blocked by the house's shadow on the West side. What is the name of the factor in your observations that affected the tomato plants growth?

    a. The control
    b. The independent variable
    c. The dependent variable
    d. The conclusion

7. There are three insects that are being compared under a microscope. As a scientist, you decide that measuring them would be an important part of recording their data. Which unit of measurement would best for this situation?

    a. Centimeters
    b. Meters
    c. Micrometers
    d. Kilometers

8. A leading drug company has created a drug that can help cure diabetes, but before it can go on the market, the company must first prove that it works. The scientists use the drug on a group of 100 people and provide a placebo to another 100 people; neither group knows if they have received the drug or the placebo. All other factors, such as exercise, diet, and amount of sleep, have stayed the same. What is this experiment using to determine if the drug works?

    a. A standard deviation
    b. A dependent variable
    c. A hypothesis
    d. A control group

9. Which of the following is not provided as a result of the valid research and observations recorded by scientists?

    a. A better understanding of the physical world
    b. The ability to predict possible outcomes affected by actions
    c. The ability to prevent earthquakes and other natural disasters
    d. The creation of various substances and technologies that enhance our world

Question 10 pertains to the following table:

State Coyote Population, 1900-2010			
Year	Population	Year	Population
1900	5,000	1960	50,000
1910	11,000	1970	70,000
1920	30,000	1980	50,000

1930	75,000	1990	40,000
1940	100,000	2000	20,000
1950	65,000	2010	8,000

10. In reference to the above table, if the state allowed hunting in only the highest populated years, what conclusions below would not have affected the continued decrease in population numbers from 1970 to 2010?

    a. Scarcity of food sources
    b. Migration to another area
    c. The prohibition of coyote hunting
    d. Reduction of shelter

11. In 1912, Alfred Wegener proposed that:

    a. The earth's magnetic poles have reversed several times throughout history
    b. Tectonic plates move because of convection currents in the mantle
    c. Mountains are formed by tectonic plates pushing against one another
    d. The continents once formed a single land mass, but have since drifted apart

12. While doing a chemistry experiment during class one of your friends gets splashed in the eye with a solution that you were mixing. What is the first thing you should do to help your friend?

    a. Tell the teacher
    b. Take your friend to the eyewash
    c. Tell them to blink and that everything will be fine
    d. Tell them to rub their eyes and then tell the teacher

13. What are goggles, lab aprons, and gloves called?

    a. People protective equines
    b. Personal protect equipment
    c. Personal protective equipment
    d. People protective equipment

14. After a laboratory experiment that involved using various chemical solutions, you and your lab partner are asked to clean up your workspace and dispose of any leftover chemicals. Unsure about the appropriate disposal method, you refer to which manual to find the best method for each solution?

    a. Maternal Data Shifting Sheet
    b. Maternal Data Safety Sheet
    c. Materials Don't Shift Sheet
    d. Safety Data Sheet

Question 15 pertains to the following diagram:

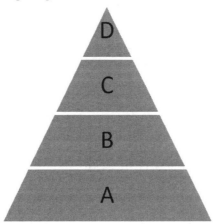

15. In the food chain pyramid above, which segment represents the placement of a coyote?

    a. A (Producer)
    b. B (Primary Consumer)
    c. C (Secondary Consumer)
    d. D (Decomposer)

16. All living things have:

    a. Organelles
    b. Cells
    c. Tissues
    d. Cell walls

17. The Gulf Oil Spill of 2010 deposited millions of gallons of crude oil into the wetlands of Louisiana, and many people in the area suffered. Which of the factors below was not among those drastically affected by the oil spill?

    a. Water quality
    b. Water temperature
    c. Air quality
    d. Presence of fish

18. What is the name of the process by which plants generate their own food source using sunlight, carbon dioxide, and water?

    a. Photoemission
    b. Chemotherapy
    c. Chemosynthesis
    d. Photosynthesis

19. In the marine waters, there is a beautiful, orange clown fish that lives closely with a sea anemone. This sea anemone can sting its prey with poisonous venom before devouring it; however, the clown fish is not affected by the sea anemone at all. The clown fish is only safe when hiding within the sea anemone's poisonous tentacles and protects the hiding spot from a certain type of fish who tries to eat the sea anemone. This is an example of what type of relationship?

    a. Commensalism
    b. Mutualism
    c. Parasitism
    d. None of the above

20. The sun provides a source of light for our planet, but it also plays an important role by heating the air and water, in turn causing atmospheric winds and ocean currents. The sun heats the air and water by _____.

    a. Conduction
    b. Radiation
    c. Convection
    d. None of the above

21. Which of the following is the most likely explanation for the reason finches on separate islands within an archipelago have differently shaped beaks?

    a. Each bird evolved from a pre-existing ancestor on each island
    b. The finches spread among the islands, but in small numbers, so genetic drift caused beak shape to change
    c. Natural selection shaped the beaks in accordance with food availability on each island
    d. The different finches were introduced by ancient humans

Question 22 pertains to the following diagram:

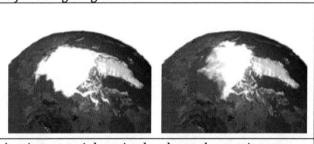

Arctic perennial sea ice has been decreasing at a rate of 9% per decade. The first image shows the minimum sea ice concentration for the year 1979, and the second image shows the minimum sea ice concentration in 2003.

22. The above images show the Arctic Circle in 1979 and in 2003. Which of the following would not be a short- or long-term effect of this change?

    a. Impact on the ecological food pyramids and webs
    b. Increase in sea levels
    c. Diminished wetlands and marshes around the world
    d. Decreased global temperatures for the land and oceans

23. Which of the following situations would result in the generation of new crust?

    a. Two crustal plates converge
    b. Two crustal plates move apart
    c. Two crustal plates slide past one another
    d. A crustal plate is pushed down into the mantle

24. Which of the following is a property of nonmetals?

    a. They are good conductors of electricity
    b. They do not form isotopes
    c. They react with metals
    d. They are dense, hard, and have high melting points

25. The moon plays an important role in which of the following earth events?

    a. Tides
    b. Earthquakes
    c. Earth's orbit
    d. Northern Lights

26. The average distance from the earth to the sun is equal to one:

    a. Astronomical unit
    b. Light year
    c. Parsec
    d. Arcsecond

27. On your way to school you are carrying a book bag full of academic supplies, books, and lunch. What is causing the book bag to begin to feel very heavy as you walk to school?

    a. The mass of the book bag
    b. The weight of the book bag
    c. The volume of the book bag
    d. The size of the book bag

28. Cells are the smallest unit of a living organism; therefore, atoms would be the smallest unit of _____.

    a. Matter
    b. Mass
    c. Weight
    d. Periodic Table

29. Balance the following reaction between sulfuric acid and aluminum hydroxide by filling in the correct stoichiometric values for each chemical.

$$\_\ H_2SO_4 + \_\ Al(OH)_3 \rightarrow \_\ Al_2(SO_4)_3 + \_\ H_2O$$

    a. 3, 2, 1, 6
    b. 2, 3, 1, 3
    c. 3, 3, 2, 6
    d. 1, 2, 1, 4

30. What are the three main sections of the Periodic Table?

    a. Metals, nonmetals, and gases
    b. Metals, metalloids, and gases
    c. Metals, nonmetals, and metalloids
    d. Nonmetals, metalloids, and gases

31. Place your answer on the provided griddable answer sheet.

Using the Periodic Table, what is the total number of protons for iron?

32. Which answer balances the following equation?
$CO_2 + H_2O + Energy = C_6H_{12}O_6 + O_2$

    a. $12CO_2 + 6H_2O + Energy = C_6H_{12}O_6 + 6O_2$
    b. $6CO_2 + 6H_2O + Energy = 2C_6H_{12}O_6 + 12O_2$
    c. $12CO_2 + 6H_2O + Energy = 2C_6H_{12}O_6 + 6O_2$
    d. $6CO_2 + 6H_2O + Energy = C_6H_{12}O_6 + 6O_2$

33. Place your answer on the provided griddable answer sheet.

You are driving to your grandmother's house for her birthday. She lives 582 miles away. The average speed limit is 65mph. How long will it take you to get to your grandmother's house?

34. Most organic molecules have all of the following properties except

    a. High solubility in water
    b. A tendency to melt
    c. Covalently bonded
    d. High flammability

35. You are getting on a train bound for New York City, and your return trip will track at the same rate of speed. If you were going to determine your velocity, what would you need to know in addition to the speed of the trains?

    a. Acceleration
    b. Force
    c. Direction
    d. Reference point

36. A cheetah at rest is initially at 0m/s and then gets up to 2m/s once it begins to chase after an antelope. What is this change in velocity called?

    a. Speed
    b. Direction
    c. Acceleration
    d. Inertia

37. Which of the following is an example of a balanced force?

    a. Two football players grabbing a football from the same direction
    b. Two football players pushing on a football from opposite directions
    c. A football player kicking the ball
    d. A football player throwing the ball

38. Place your answer on the provided griddable answer sheet.

While driving in a car as a passenger, your mother stops abruptly in order to avoid hitting a hubcap in the road. After she slams on her brakes, you both move forward and then back once the seatbelt is activated. This is an example of which of Newton's Laws?

39. If the moon is at the point in its cycle where it is between the earth and the sun, which moon phase would we observe from the earth?

    a. New moon
    b. Last moon
    c. Full moon
    d. First quarter moon

40. When a cold front begins to overtake a warm front, this results in what type of front?

    a. Stationary front
    b. Occluded front
    c. Cold front
    d. Warm front

41. All of the following are examples of chemical changes in the digestive system except

    a. Converting starches in carbohydrates to simple sugars
    b. Protein digestion in the stomach
    c. Chewing food into smaller pieces
    d. Digestion of fat in the small intestine

42. The reason for seasonal changes on earth is because of the earth's revolution around the sun and which unique aspect of the earth?

    a. The earth rotates around the moon
    b. The earth is tilted at its equator
    c. The earth is tilted at its axis
    d. None of these

43. Many fishermen will watch the tide report for the local area and get up very early or stay out late in order to have the best fishing opportunity. Which factor affects the fisherman's fishing opportunities?

    a. The gravitational relationship between the earth and moon
    b. The gravitational relationship between the earth and sun
    c. The earth's gravity
    d. The moon's phases

44. In an amusement park ride, you stand on the floor of a cylindrical ring with your back touching the wall. The ring begins to rotate, slowly at first, but then faster and faster. When the ring is rotating fast enough, the floor is removed. You do not slide down but remained pressed against the wall of the ring. Which is the best explanation for why you don't fall down?

    a. The centripetal force pushes you towards the wall
    b. The centripetal force changes the direction of your motion
    c. The force of friction between the wall and your body is greater than your weight
    d. The rotating ring creates a weightless environment

Question 45 pertains to the following diagram:

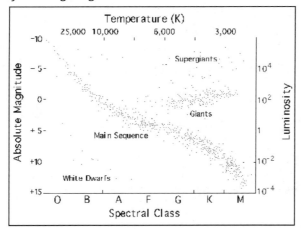

45. What is the name of the above figure used to classify stars based on temperature and luminosity?

    a. Hershbrown-Russell diagram
    b. Hertzsprung-Russell diagram
    c. Hersheysrug-Russell diagram
    d. None of the above

46. Place your answer on the provided griddable answer sheet.

100 g of ethanol C_2H_6O is dissolved in 100 g of water. The final solution has a volume of 0.2 L. What is the density of the resulting solution?

47. Identify the leaf shown below using the provided dichotomous key:

————————Step 1————————			
Is the leaf round?	Go to Step 2	Is the leaf long and skinny?	It is a Black Walnut

————————Step 2————————			
Does the leaf have smooth edges?	Go to Step 3	Does the leaf have saw tooth edges?	It is a Mulberry

————————Step 3————————			
Does the leaf have no lobes (fingers)?	It is a Dogwood	Does the leaf have lobes (fingers)?	It is a Sassafras

The leaf shown in the pictures is:
   a. Black Walnut
   b. Mulberry
   c. Dogwood
   d. Sassafras

48. Electromagnetic waves provide scientists with a way to determine the distance of an object by emitting pulses of radio waves and waiting for them to hit something in their path and bounce back. Which relation would you use to determine the distance of the object from the emitter?
   a. Distance = mass/velocity
   b. Force = mass * acceleration
   c. Speed = distance/time
   d. Work = Force * distance

- 49 -

49. When an animal takes in more energy that it uses over an extended time, the extra chemical energy is stored as:

    a. Fat
    b. Starch
    c. Protein
    d. Enzymes

50. What is primary driving force in the development a hurricane?

    a. High winds
    b. Ocean temperatures
    c. Cloud cover
    d. Contact with land

51. Prokaryotic and eukaryotic cells are similar in having which of the following?

    a. Membrane-bound organelles
    b. Protein-studded DNA
    c. Presence of a nucleus
    d. Integral membrane proteins in the plasma membrane

52. Which of the following organisms is capable of undergoing asexual reproduction?

    a. Ferns
    b. Yeast
    c. Flowering plants
    d. Trees

53. The brain is part of the:

    a. Integumentary system
    b. Nervous system
    c. Endocrine system
    d. Respiratory system

54. Genetics is the study of:

    a. Anatomy
    b. Physiology
    c. Heredity
    d. Science

Answers and Explanations

1. A: Temperature affects a molecule in two ways. Hotter temperatures cause molecules expand and move apart from each other; colder temperatures make them shrink and pull together, just like you would on a cold day. The answer is (A) because the mercury molecules will expand on a hotter day, causing the mercury to rise up the thermometer.

2. D: Students should know where to locate a fire extinguisher should a small fire should start. If it is too large to contain, they should immediately exit the building and call 911. Students should wear lab coats and safety goggles to protect clothing and eyes from any spillage of the substance and to reduce the chance of it getting into their eyes. Rubber boots would not be as protective as the lab coat and goggles.

3. C: A trend is the foreseeable pattern of an observed event. In this case, the students began to observe the teacher giving a quiz every Monday covering the material presented two weeks prior; therefore, they observed a trend.

4. A: According to the table, Jacob started with a 70% and has consistently moved up 10% with each quarter, as has Kate, but she started at 60%. Samantha started at 55% and has not always increased her scores. Should this trend continue, Jacob will most likely earn a 100%.

5. A: The table reflects student scores for each quarter. The trend that can be seen in the graph is an increase in scores as the year progressed. The graph label mentions a test review, but there is not enough information about that to know if that is the reason for the scores changing.

6. B: The conclusion was that the amount of sunlight received by the plants was affecting their growth. The independent variable was the amount of light that was given to the plants and could have been manipulated by the experimenter by moving the plants or adding equal parts of light. No control was used in this experiment.

7. C: The best use of the International System of Units (SI) for this situation would be the use of the micrometer as it is the smallest unit of measurement provided and the scientist is using a microscope to view the insects.

8. D: The drug company has provided all of the same variables to the two groups with the exception of one group receiving the drug and the other taking the placebo. The group on the drug is experimental; the placebo is a control group.

9. C: Scientists make observations, gather data, and complete research over many years in order to compile knowledge that will provide insight into future disasters, such as earthquakes, storms, and global warming. Although science can be used to predict earthquakes and other natural disasters, there is currently no way of preventing them from occurring.

10. C: Although no data is shown that reflects the years in which hunting licenses were sold, the prohibition of hunting would allow a population to increase its numbers. The coyote's populations would suffer without adequate food sources or shelter, and migration would reduce it as well.

11. D: In 1912, Alfred Wegener proposed that the continents once formed a single land mass called Pangaea, but have since drifted apart. Theories about the earth's magnetic fields and plate tectonics did not emerge until years later. Once they did, they helped produce evidence to support Wegener's theory.

12. B: The first thing you should do is assist your friend to the eyewash. After, or if possible while, doing this, you should get the attention of the teacher. Depending on the solution that was introduced into the eye, every second counts to maintain the integrity of the eye itself and its vision. Rubbing or blinking may further irritate the eye and cause more damage.

13. C: Goggles, lab aprons, and gloves are personal protective equipment for an individual to wear as protection against splashing solutions onto clothing or skin or into the eyes and should be worn while working with any chemicals or flammable materials.

14. D: While some chemicals can be poured down the drain safely without affecting the pipes or the environment, not all can. Therefore, by reading about the chemical in the Safety Data Sheet (SDS), you can determine if it is caustic, flammable, or harmful to the environment if poured down the drain.

15. C: The diagram represents an ecological pyramid. The letter A represents the producers, such as plants. The letter B represents the primary consumers usually herbivores. The letter C stands for the secondary consumers, the carnivores that feed on the herbivores. A coyote is a carnivore and would, therefore, be in this group and represented by the letter C. The pyramid's fourth level, represented by a D, includes the decomposers, such as bacteria and fungi, which decompose dead organic material.

16. B: Cells are the basic units of life, and all organisms have them. Some organisms like bacteria have just a single cell, while complex organisms like humans have hundreds of trillions. Prokaryotes do not have organelles Not all organisms have tissues, groups of cells that make up connective tissue, muscle tissue, etc. Finally, only some types of cells, including plant cells, have cell walls d.

17. B: All of the factors above were drastically affected by the oil spill except the temperature of the water. Oil did not significantly impact the temperature of the water. The spill did impact the water quality and air quality by the introduction of oil and other chemicals from the cleanup into the water and air. The presence of the oil also killed or drove away many of the fish that would otherwise have been near the gulf coast.

18. D: Photosynthesis is the process by which plants generate their own food (glucose), using sunlight, water, and carbon dioxide. Oxygen is also generated as a byproduct.

19. B: The relationship between the clown fish and the sea anemone is an example of mutualism - because both organisms are benefitting from the relationship. The Clown fish gains the protection from the anemone while offering protection to the anemone from being eaten by a certain type of fish.

20. B: Radiation is the heat energy that is transferred from electromagnetic waves such as the sun. Convection is the transfer of heat energy within a gas or liquid substance because of circulation. Conduction is the transfer of heat by direct contact. Once the air and water have been heated, they move and circulate because of the difference in the density of hot and cold water and of hot and cold air.

21. C: Finches with beaks well-suited for the types of food available on an island had an evolutionary advantage. As a result, these finches survived and reproduced, a phenomenon known as natural selection. The finches share a common ancestor, regardless of the island on which they now live. Genetic drift refers to genetic changes that occur due to random chance; this would not

- 52 -

account for different beaks on different islands. Introduction by humans would not account for different beaks, since phenotypes change over time.

22. D: The melting of the Arctic Circle would mean that sea levels would increase and wetlands and marshes would then become flooded with seawater. This would lead to the death of many plant and animal species within those ecosystems. Global temperatures would not decrease but would increase on both the land and oceans.

23. B: Two crustal plates move apart. When two crustal plates move apart, magma welling up could result in the formation of new crust. This has been shown to be occurring on the ocean floor where places of the crust are weaker. The crust spreads apart at these trenches, pushing outward and erupting at the ridges. When two crustal plates converge, sublimation occurs as one plate runs under another pushing it up. Two crustal plates slide past one another, is an example of a transform fault, which does not create new crust. A crustal plate is pushed down into the mantle, does not form new crust but perhaps recycles the old one.

24. C: Nonmetal ions are negatively charged, while metal ions are positively charged. Because of these opposite charges, they readily bond and react. The metal iron, for instance, reacts readily with the nonmetal oxygen to form rust. As a general rule, nonmetals are considered nonconductors Nonmetals, including oxygen, can form isotopes. Nonmetals typically have low densities, are not hard, and have low melting points.

25. A: The moon's gravitational pull against the earth causes the earth's oceans to bulge out at the points nearest to and farthest from the moon, causing the displacement of water that occurs twice a day, known as high and low tide.

26. A: The average distance from the earth to the sun is equal to one astronomical unit. An astronomical unit (AU) is equal to 93 million miles, and is far smaller than a light year or a parsec. A light year is defined as the distance light can travel in a vacuum in one year, and is equal to roughly 64,341 AU. A parsec is the parallax of one arcsecond, and is equal to 206.26×10^3 astronomical units.

27. B: Weight and mass are very similar but differ in that mass is the amount of matter something contains and can be measured in grams and weight is affected by the gravitational pull of the object. Weight is the answer because gravity is pulling on the book bag, making it feel heavier than it really is.

28. A: Atoms are the smallest and most basic unit of matter. When combined, they form elements just as cells of the same type form tissues.

29. A: By comparing the products to the reactants, there must be at least two Al atoms in the starting material, and at least three sulfate groups. Therefore, a coefficient of 2 must be placed in front of $Al(OH)_3$ and a coefficient of 3 must be placed in front of H_2SO_4. To make the number of hydrogen and oxygen atoms equal on both sides of the equation, a coefficient of 6 must be placed in front of H_2O.

30. C: The Periodic Table systematically arranges elements according to their properties, and many of the properties are more reactive than others. The most reactive are the metals, which are found on the left side of the table. The least reactive are the nonmetals, found on the right. In between the metals and nonmetals are the metalloids, which share some of the properties of both groups.

31. 26: On the Periodic Table, iron (Fe) has an atomic number of 26 and an atomic mass of 55.847. The atomic number indicates the number of protons that the element has within its nucleus. The atomic mass is the average mass of the isotopes within that element. The answer is 26 protons because the atomic number is 26.

32. D: The equation $6CO_2 + 6H_2O + Energy = C_6H_{12}O_6 + 6O_2$ (photosynthesis) can be balanced by counting the number of each element on the reactant side and comparing those totals to the product side. There should be equal numbers of each element on both sides, and they can be adjusted by changing the coefficient to add another molecule to the formula to balance the other side. The formula above represents photosynthesis and has six more CO_2 molecules on its reactant side than usual; thus, additional glucose and oxygen molecules will be produced.

33. 9 hours: The formula for calculating speed is S=D/T. However, you are looking for time, so you would divide distance (D) by speed (S) to get the time (T). The answer is 9 hours.

34. A: high solubility in water. Most organic molecules have all of the following properties except high solubility in water. A tendency to melt, covalently bonded, and high flammability, are all characteristics of organic molecules. Organic molecules are those that contain carbon molecules, with a few exceptions. Organic molecules tend to be less soluble in water than inorganic salts. They are good at forming unique structures and there are many organic compounds. Examples of organic compounds include hydrocarbons, carbohydrates, lipids and proteins.

35. C: Velocity is the speed of an object going in a specific direction; therefore, the answer is direction.

36. C: Acceleration is the change in an object's velocity. Velocity is the direction and speed in which an object is moving.

37. B: A balanced force is one that has no net force being applied to an object; therefore, it does not move. The two football players that are pushing on the football from opposite directions are applying force from both sides so that the ball does not move, making it a balanced force.

38. First: Newton's First Law is the law of inertia, which states an object will continue in the direction that it was traveling until acted upon. In this case, your body continued to move forward until your seatbelt stopped you, acting as an unbalanced force.

39. A: A new moon is one that is in between the earth and sun. The moon would then receive light on the side closest to the sun and its illuminated sides would not be directly visible to us on the earth.

40. B: An occluded front occurs when a cold front has overtaken a warm front, resulting in a mature storm system. A stationary front does not move. A cold front brings cold air, while a warm front brings warm air.

41. C: Chewing food into smaller pieces is a physical change, not a chemical change.

42. C: The earth experiences seasons because it revolves around the sun while tilted on its axis, exposing one hemisphere to the sun more than the other hemisphere. The hemisphere closest to the sun will be experiencing summer, while the other hemisphere has winter. The Northern Hemisphere and Southern Hemisphere experience opposite seasons all year long.

43. A: The rising and falling of the ocean's tides are directly influenced by the gravitational pull of the moon on the earth. High tide is found in areas closest and farthest from the moon because the moon pulls the water and earth toward it, leaving the water on the other side of the earth behind. Low tide occurs in the areas not affected by high tide. There are two tides each day.

44. C: The centripetal force pushes you in toward the center of the ring, not towards the wall. The centripetal force also causes the ring to push against you, which is why it might feel like you're being pushed outwards. This force also causes friction between your back and the wall, and that is why you don't fall when the floor is removed, assuming the frictional force is large enough to overcome gravity. As the speed of rotation increases, the force exerted by the wall on your body increases, so the frictional force between you and the wall increases. Centripetal force does cause you to change direction—but it does not explain why you don't fall. Also note that "centrifugal force" is an illusion; because you feel the wall pushing against your back, you feel like you're being pushed outwards. In fact, you're being pulled inwards, but the wall is also being pulled inwards and is pushing against you. Finally, you are not weightless on a ride like this.

45. B: The Hertzsprung-Russell diagram was named after the designers Ejnar Hertzsprung and Henry Norris Russell. The diagram plots stars based on their spectral class or temperature and magnitude or luminosity.

46. 1 g/mL: Density is determined by dividing the mass of the solution by its volume. The mass is 200 g, and the total volume is 0.2 L, or 200 mL. So 200 g/200 mL = 1 g/mL.

47. B: A mulberry leaf is round in shape and has saw tooth edges. Following the dichotomous key helps to identify the leaf based on its physical characteristics.

48. C: The formula for calculating speed is distance over time. Since we know the speed of the waves and the time it took to get to the object and back, we can calculate the distance.

49. A: Long term energy storage in animals takes the form of fat. Animals also store energy as glycogen, and plants store energy as starch, but these substances are for shorter-term use. Fats are a good storage form for chemical energy because fatty acids bond to glycerol in a condensation reaction to form fats (triglycerides). This reaction, which releases water, allows for the compacting of high-energy fatty acids in a concentrated form.

50. B: Hurricanes are primarily formed because of the temperature difference between the oceans and the atmospheric air. The oceans heat up during the summer months and once they climb above 80 degrees Fahrenheit, the conditions are ideal for a hurricane. Evaporation of the warm water forms clouds, which then expand into storm clouds. Atmospheric winds help push the storm over warmer waters, allowing it to grow. A hurricane will die if introduced to cold waters or cut off from a water source.

51. D: Both prokaryotes and eukaryotes interact with the extracellular environment and use membrane-bound or membrane-associated proteins to achieve this. They both use diffusion and active transport to move materials in and out of their cells. Prokaryotes have very few proteins associated with their DNA, whereas eukaryotes' DNA is richly studded with proteins. Both types of living things can have flagella, although with different structural characteristics in the two groups. The most important differences between prokaryotes and eukaryotes are the lack of a nucleus and membrane-bound organelles in prokaryotes.

52. B: Asexual reproduction means that offspring are produced by a single parent. Yeast cells reproduce asexually through budding. The genetic material of the cell is copied, and a small bud forms on the outside of the yeast cell. It grows and eventually breaks away, forming a new yeast cell. Most organisms, including ferns, flowering plants, and trees, require two parents to produce seeds, spores, etc. In other words, they are not capable of asexual reproduction.

53. B: The brain is part of the nervous system.

54. C: Genetics is the study of heredity.

Practice Test #2

Practice Questions

1. Which of the following elements are ordered from least reactive to most reactive according to the Periodic Table?
 a. Ar, Cu, Na
 b. Na, Ar, Cu
 c. Na, Cu, Ar
 d. Ar, Na, Cu

2. The group of elements that contains most of the semiconductors is called?
 a. Metals
 b. Metalloids
 c. Nonmetals
 d. Noble gases

3. Place your answer on the provided griddable answer sheet.

In the chemical formula for glucose, $5C_6H_{12}O_6$, which number represents a coefficient?

4. Which of the following answers shows $CH_4 + O_2 = CO_2 + H_2O$ as balanced?
 a. $CH_4 + 2O_2 = 2CO_2 + 2H_2O$
 b. $2CH_4 + 4O_2 = 2CO_2 + H_2O$
 c. $2CH_4 + O_2 = 2CO_2 + H_2O$
 d. $CH_4 + 2O_2 = CO_2 + 2H_2O$

5. Identify the leaf shown below using the provided dichotomous key:

——————————Step 1——————————			
Is the leaf irregular, but symmetrical?	Go to Step 2	Is the leaf long and skinny?	It is a Black Walnut

——————————Step 2——————————			
Does the leaf have smooth edges?	Go to Step 3	Does the leaf have saw tooth edges?	It is a Mulberry

——————————Step 3——————————			
Does the leaf have no lobes (fingers)?	It is a Dogwood	Does the leaf have lobes (fingers)?	It is a Sassafras

The leaf shown in the pictures is:

    a. Black Walnut
    b. Mulberry
    c. Dogwood
    d. Sassafras

6. Evidence of a chemical reaction can be determined by all of the following except?

    a. Modifying the arrangement of atoms
    b. Endothermic and exothermic reactions
    c. Equal masses of reactants and products
    d. No change in energy

7. Two boys on skateboards decide to race to the end of the street. Both travel the same distance but arrive at different times. This example illustrates which concept?

    a. Direction
    b. Acceleration
    c. Speed
    d. Velocity

8. Place your answer on the provided griddable answer sheet.

Aubrey lives 200m from Brianna's house. If it takes her 100s to travel the distance, what is Aubrey's speed?

9. Which of the following devices changes chemical energy into electrical energy?

    a. Battery
    b. Closed electric circuit
    c. Generator
    d. Transformer

10. In the store, you are pushing a cart with no problem. However, as you are shopping, you add items to the cart that have varying masses. Which of Newton's Laws play a role in the amount of force needed to push the cart through the store?

    a. Newton's First Law
    b. Newton's Second Law
    c. Newton's Third Law
    d. Newton's Fourth Law

11. You are watching the Olympic ice skating championships and see the pairs are up next. They begin their routine facing each other with their palms up and against each other. When the music starts they push themselves apart with their palms. What type of force is this?

    a. Magnetic
    b. Balanced
    c. Action and reaction force
    d. Centripetal force

12. Two rabbits are getting ready to jump across the field away from a predator. One of the rabbits is about twice the size of the other. As they bound away, which of the rabbits will have to exert more force on its jumps and why?

    a. The smaller rabbit, because its legs are shorter
    b. The smaller rabbit, because it will have to take more jumps to escape the predator
    c. The larger rabbit, because it has more mass that must overcome gravity and accelerate
    d. The larger rabbit, because it has more air resistance to deal with

13. Light waves are an example of which type of wave?

    a. Longitudinal
    b. Transverse
    c. Compressional
    d. None of the above

14. Place your answer on the provided griddable answer sheet.

Substance A has a density of 5.0 kg/m³ and substance B has a density of 4.0 kg/m³. What is the ratio of the volume of A to the volume of B when the masses of the two substances are equal? Write your answer as a fraction or a decimal.

15. Which of the following is an example of visible light that travels through space and produces heat?

    a. Bioluminescence light
    b. Incandescent light
    c. Sunlight
    d. Fluorescent light

16. Which of the following is not an example of a renewable resource?

    a. Sunlight
    b. Crude oil
    c. Wind
    d. Tide

17. Coral reefs are an important ecosystem within the world's oceans. They act as a filtering system, reduce the amount of carbon dioxide in the water, provide shelter for many organisms, and offer economic benefits to many people around the world. However, coral reefs are in danger of being irreversibly destroyed. Which of the following is not a cause of the destruction of coral reefs?

    a. Reattachment of salvaged coral colonies on the reef
    b. Global warming
    c. Collection of coral by people to sell
    d. Water pollution

18. The sun sits on the edge of which galaxy?

    a. Milky Way
    b. Elliptical Galaxy
    c. Irregular Galaxy
    d. Doppler Galaxy

Question 20 pertains to the following table:

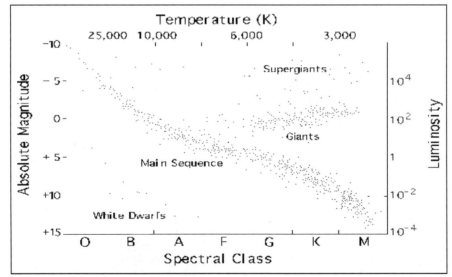

19. According to the diagram above, what unit of measurement is used to determine the star temperature?

    a. Celsius
    b. Kelvin
    c. Fahrenheit
    d. None of the above

20. Which of the following is a star with an absolute magnitude of +10 and a temperature of 25,000K?

    a. Main Sequence
    b. Super Giant
    c. Giant
    d. White Dwarf

21. Which statement correctly states the work-energy theorem?

    a. The change in kinetic energy of an object is equal to the work done by the object
    b. The change in kinetic energy of an object is equal to the work done on an object
    c. The change in potential energy of an object is equal to the work done by the object
    d. The change in potential energy of an object is equal to the work done on an object

22. Which of the following below is not considered evidence of plate tectonics?

    a. The shape of continents fits together like a puzzle
    b. Fossil comparisons exist along where the continents would fit together
    c. The Mid-Atlantic Ridge shows where new crust is formed
    d. There is a large amount of inland seismic activity

23. Earth's oceans have many little waves that are caused by the various wind speeds around the globe. However, one type of wave is caused by a celestial body. Which celestial body causes this wave?

    a. Sun
    b. Stars
    c. Planets
    d. Moon

24. On December 22 of every year, the people in the southern hemisphere of the earth experience which event?

    a. Summer Solstice
    b. Winter Solstice
    c. Spring Equinox
    d. Fall Equinox

25. The atomic number of an element is determined by:

    a. The number of neutrons in the nucleus of an atom
    b. The number of protons in the nucleus of an atom
    c. The number of protons plus the number of neutrons in an atom
    d. The number of protons plus the number of electrons in an atom

26. A tapeworm lives within another organism and feeds off the nutrients that are ingested by that organism. At times, this can cause the organism to experience malnutrition or death. This is an example of what type of relationship?

    a. Predator/prey
    b. Symbiosis
    c. Parasite/host
    d. Producer/consumer

27. In a pond, eutrophication, the pollution of water by plant nutrients, can occur, causing chemical, biological, and ecological changes to the pond. As plant material begins to decompose and carbon dioxide begins to increase, what would happen to the fish in the pond?

    a. They would flourish
    b. They would relocate to another area
    c. They would die off
    d. They would not be affected

28. In Lake Erie, a species of fish called the Blue Pike was overfished one year. The following year, there was a pollution incident that killed off another large portion of the population. These events, combined with the previous year's overfishing of adult fish, led to the extinction of the Blue Pike species—none of the other species were affected. What happened to other fish species in the lake over time after the Blue Pike became extinct?

    a. They became extinct
    b. They were not affected by the other species' fate
    c. Their numbers increased due to lack of competition
    d. Their numbers decreased due to lack of competition

29. Our planet's oceans are experiencing climate changes, pollution, and overfishing. Which of the following answers is not a result of human activity?

    a. Diminishment of coral reefs
    b. Destruction of food webs
    c. Increased population of all species
    d. Degradation or total loss of wetlands

30. Which section of the digestive system is responsible for water reabsorption?

    a. The large intestine
    b. The duodenum
    c. The small intestine
    d. The gallbladder

31. All of the following are examples of physical changes in the digestive system except:

    a. Squeezing the food through the esophagus
    b. Drinking to help aid in swallowing food
    c. Chewing food into smaller pieces
    d. Digestion of fat in the small intestine

32. Which moon phase is the opposite moon phase of a new moon?

    a. New moon
    b. Last moon
    c. Full moon
    d. First quarter moon

33. Two species of finches are able to utilize the same food supply, but their beaks are different. They are able to coexist on an island because of:

    a. Niche overlap
    b. Character displacement
    c. Resource partitioning
    d. Realized niches

34. In mosses, eggs and sperm are produced by:

    a. Spores
    b. Sporophytes
    c. Gametophytes
    d. Zygotes

35. You and a lab partner will be completing a scientific experiment measuring the mass of chewed gum after one-minute chewing increments. Which lab equipment will you most likely use?

    a. Triple beam balance
    b. Anemometer
    c. Hot plate
    d. Microscope

36. A triple beam balance would show the units of measurement in which form?

    a. Liters
    b. Grams
    c. Meters
    d. Gallons

37. All of the following are examples of controlling eukaryotic gene expression EXCEPT

    a. Regulatory proteins
    b. Nucleosome packing
    c. Methylation of DNA
    d. Operons

38. Mrs. Jones's class conducted an experiment on the effects of sugar and artificial sweetener on the cookie recipe's overall color when baked. What would be the independent variable in the cookie experiment?

    a. The students should use the same ingredients in both recipes, but bake the cookies with sugar at 450 degrees and those with artificial sweetener at 475 degrees. They should increase the baking time on the artificial sweetener cookies, since the package instructs them to do so
    b. The students should use the same ingredients in both recipes, but increase the baking time on the artificial sweetener cookies, since the package instructs them to do so
    c. The students should use the same ingredients, same baking temperatures, and same baking times for both recipes
    d. The students should use the same ingredients and baking times in both recipes, but bake the cookies with sugar at 450 degrees and the artificial sweetener cookies at 475 degrees

39. In the suburban neighborhood of Northwoods, there have been large populations of deer, and residents have complained about them eating flowers and garden plants. What would be a logical explanation, based on observations, for the large increase in the deer population over the last two seasons?

    a. Increased quantity of food sources
    b. Decreased population of a natural predator
    c. Deer migration from surrounding areas
    d. Increase in hunting licenses sold

Questions 40-42 pertain to the following passage:

Your class is competing with another class to determine who has the best plant color. Your class decides to test a couple of solutions to determine which would be best for overall plant color before competing. The class decides to water the plants once a week with 200ml of the following solutions: water, diet soda, 1% bleach solution, and a 1% salt solution. All plants are placed in the window that receives the recommended amount of light. After a month of testing, your class notices that only two plants are alive, but one of those two does not look healthy.

40. What is the independent control used in the plant color experiment?

a. 200 ml quantity of solution
b. Amount of sunlight provided
c. Number of times the plants are watered
d. The type of solution applied to the plants

41. Based on the results that were stated, what would be a logical reason for some of the plants dying with the salt solution?

a. Salt caused the plants to begin to dry up, causing them to die.
b. The salt did not affect the plants.
c. The salt provided adequate nutrients for color.
d. None of the above

42. What is the control, if any, in this experiment?

a. There is no control in this experiment
b. The control is the water
c. The control is the diet soda
d. The control is the amount of sunlight provided to the plants

43. What is a hypothetical explanation for an occurrence that is based on prior knowledge called?

a. Independent variable
b. Dependent variable
c. Trial
d. Hypothesis

44. What lab equipment would most likely be used to measure a liquid solution?

a. Flask
b. Triple beam balance
c. Graduated cylinder
d. Test tube

45. Which answer below represents the first steps in the scientific investigation process?

a. Construct a hypothesis and test with experiment
b. Analyze results and draw conclusions
c. Report results
d. Ask a question about a problem and do background research

46. During a chemistry experiment, which of the data below would not be collected for your lab report?

    a. Temperature changes
    b. Color changes
    c. Production of gas or odor
    d. Observations of other trials

47. What preventative safety equipment is required when working with flammable materials?

    a. Apron
    b. Fire blanket and extinguisher
    c. Eye wash station
    d. Goggles

48. What kind of graph would be best to represent data from an experiment with repeated trials comparing the speed of a car and the distance it traveled over time?

    a. Pie graph
    b. Bar graph
    c. Line graph
    d. Scatter plot graph

Question 49 pertains to the following chart:

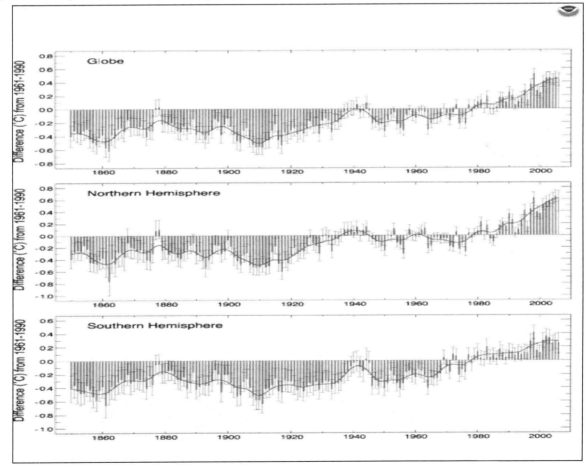

49. The above data table shows the increase of global warming from 1860 to 2000. Which portion of the globe has had the most effect on global warming?

  a. Southern Hemisphere
  b. Northern Hemisphere
  c. Western Hemisphere
  d. Eastern Hemisphere

50. The part of the human excretory system most responsible for maintaining normal body temperature is the:

  a. Kidney
  b. Bladder
  c. Liver
  d. Sweat glands

51. Of the following, which is the most basic unit of matter?

  a. A helium atom
  b. A sodium ion
  c. A proton
  d. An oxygen molecule

52. Which of the following is not true for all cells?

  a. Cells are the basic structures of any organism
  b. Cells can only reproduce from existing cells
  c. Cells are the smallest unit of any life form that carries the information needed for all life processes
  d. All cells are also called eukaryotes

53. In which of the following scenarios is Mario not applying work to a book?

  a. Mario moves a book from the floor to the top shelf of a bookcase
  b. Mario lets go of a book that he is holding so that it falls to the floor
  c. Mario pushes a box of books across the room
  d. Mario balances a book on his head and walks across the room

54. Place your answer on the provided griddable answer sheet.

You blow up a rubber balloon and hold the opening tight with your fingers. You then release your fingers, causing air to blow out of the balloon. This pushes the balloon forward, causing the balloon shoots across the room. Which of Newton's laws best explains the cause of this motion?

Answers and Explanations

1. A: The Periodic Table's two most reactive groups are Group 1 and Group 17; therefore, Na, found in Group 1, would be the most reactive of the three elements. The element Cu is found in Group 11, which marks it as a transition metal, and is only somewhat reactive. Group 18, which includes Ar, contains the Noble Gases, which are not at all reactive.

2. B: An element that has semi-conductive properties would be a metalloid. Metals are good conductors of electricity and heat. In contrast, nonmetals and the noble gases are not good conductors of electricity and heat. A semi-conductor is one that will conduct electricity under some conditions, but not others.

3. 5: In the formula for glucose, the numbers 6 and 12 both represent subscripts. A subscript represents the number of molecules for that specific element present in the formula. The C, H, and O are symbols for the elements Carbon, Hydrogen, and Oxygen, respectively. A coefficient is the number in front of the formula and represents the total number of molecules; in this formula there are five glucose molecules.

4. D: For the formula $CH_4 + O_2 = CO_2 + H_2O$ to be balanced there must be an equal number of molecules on both the reactant and product sides. In this case, for the formula to be balanced, a coefficient of a 2 needs to be placed in front of the O_2 and the H_2O molecules.

5. D: A sassafras leaf is irregular in shape but symmetrical. It also has smooth edges and finger like lobes. Following the dichotomous key helps to identify the leaf based on its physical characteristics.

6. D: A chemical reaction will always have an endothermic (absorb energy) or exothermic (release energy) reaction, and a chemical formula must always be balanced. Therefore, the masses of the reactants and products will always be equal, resulting in the modification of the atoms arrangement and a change in energy.

7. C: Speed is the distance at which something travels within a given time. The example states that both skateboarders traveled the same distance but arrived at different time. Therefore, they traveled at different speeds.

8. 2 m/s: The formula to calculate speed is S=D/T. In this problem, divide 200m by 100s, which gives you 2m/s.

9. A: In a Zn-Cu battery, the zinc terminal has a higher concentration of electrons than the copper terminal, so there is a potential difference between the locations of the two terminals. This is a form of electrical energy brought about by the chemical interactions between the metals and the electrolyte the battery uses. Creating a circuit and causing a current to flow will transform the electrical energy into heat energy, mechanical energy, or another form of electrical energy, depending on the devices in the circuit. A generator transforms mechanical energy into electrical energy and a transformer changes the electrical properties of a form of electrical energy.

10. B: Newton's Second Law states that the acceleration of an object is increased by the force applied and decreased by its mass. As the cart becomes heavier through the store, the shopper must apply more force when pushing it to achieve its acceleration. Newton's First Law states if an object is at rest, it will stay at rest until a force is acted upon it. Newton's Third Law states that any object that exerts a force will be met by an equal opposing force. There is no Fourth Law.

11. C: The ice skaters are applying Newton's Third Law to create an equal and opposite reaction force, causing both partners to move. Although each skater is pushing the other, there is another force that must be considered in that they moved as well.

12. C: The larger rabbit, because it has more mass that must overcome gravity and accelerate. Newton's Second Law states that the force required to accelerate a body is directly proportional to its mass. Thus, the larger rabbit will have to exert more force on the ground to achieve the same level of acceleration as the smaller rabbit.

13. B: A transverse wave is one in which the oscillation is perpendicular to the direction of motion. Light waves are made up of an electric field and magnetic field which both oscillate perpendicular to the direction of motion and to one another.

14. 4/5 or 0.8: The density of an object is its mass divided by its volume. One easy way to work this problem is to select a convenient mass for both substances and compare the volumes. If you have 20 kg of both materials, you will have 4.0 m³ of A and 5.0 m³ of B. The ratio of the volume of A to the volume of B is 4/5 or 0.8.

15. C: Sunlight is a source of visible light and produces heat that is transferred throughout space. Bioluminescence is a visible light created by living things, but it does not produce heat like incandescent lights do. Fluorescent lights are an artificial light source created by man and require electricity to function.

16. B: Renewable resources are those resources whose supplies can replenish naturally as quickly as or more quickly than they are consumed. Examples of renewable resources are sunlight, tides, and wind, which occur naturally and are plentiful. Fossil fuels take many years to form and are currently being consumed faster than they are being produced.

17. A: Coral reefs are destroyed by increased temperatures resulting from global warming and water pollution, which suffocates the coral as algae grows over it. Illegal collection and sale of coral to restaurants, pet stores, and others have depleted healthy colonies. Many conservation efforts include enacting international laws protecting the reefs, creating natural parks, and reattaching salvaged coral colonies on the reef with the hopes of reconstructing the reef have been started in recent years.

18. A: The sun is located in our galaxy, the Milky Way, which is a spiral-shaped galaxy. Elliptical and Irregular Galaxies are examples of other galaxy shapes. There is no Doppler Galaxy.

19. B: The Hertzsprung-Russell diagram uses the Kelvin International System of Units (SI) measurement to measure the temperature of a star,

20. D: White Dwarf stars are found at the lower left-hand corner of the Hertzsprung-Russell diagram and can be plotted by following the 10+ magnitude and a temperature of 25,000K until the two points meet.

21. B: The work-energy theorem can be written $W = \Delta KE$. It is derived from Newton's second law ($F = ma$) by multiplying both sides by the distance the object moves. This work is the work done by a force on an object, and not the work done by an object. Work is only done by an object if that object exerts a force on another object, causing a change in its kinetic energy or position. The work done on an object MAY equal its potential energy, but only if that potential energy is converted into kinetic energy. In real-life cases, some energy is converted to heat, for example, so the change in potential energy does not equal the change in kinetic energy.

22. D: Evidence of plate tectonics is based on the shapes of the continents, which seem to fit together like a puzzle, as well as the fossils found along these edges. The Mid-Atlantic Ridge is the birthplace of new crust that is then destroyed in the subduction zones in the Pacific Ring of Fire, where most seismic activity takes place.

23. D: Although all of the answers are celestial bodies, natural bodies outside of the earth's atmosphere, only one influences the earth's tides. The moon's gravitational pull on the earth causes the seas to rise and fall as one large wave, known as a tide, with a very large wavelength as compared to waves formed by wind.

24. A: Due to the earth's tilt on its axis, the two hemispheres experience different seasons at opposite times because when one is pointed toward the sun, the other is facing away. In the Northern Hemisphere, winter occurs in December and summer in July. In the Southern Hemisphere, it is the opposite. The two Equinoxes occur oppositely for each hemisphere as well.

25. B: The atomic number is equal to the number of protons in the nucleus, which is equal to the number of electrons. The number of protons plus the number of neutrons is equal to the mass number of the atom.

26. C: A parasite is an organism that feeds off the nutritional assets of another living thing called the host, which can lead to the host becoming malnourished or dying. Symbiosis occurs when there is a benefit to both organisms. A predator eats its prey. A producer produces food in the form of plant material that is eaten by a consumer.

27. C: In a pond, plants produce oxygen as a byproduct of photosynthesis. During eutrophication, plants die and decompose, causing increased levels of carbon dioxide. Fish cannot relocate from the pond, and they cannot live without oxygen, so they would die.

28. C: In an ecosystem, when one species is affected by overfishing or pollution, other species will either thrive due to a lack of competition or become extinct for the same reasons. The question states that the other species were not impacted by the overfishing or pollution. Thus, their populations would not have decreased for those reasons. Once extinct, the other species were no longer the potential prey of the Blue Pike or competing against them for similar food sources and so had the opportunity to increase their population numbers.

29. C: Human activities have not influenced the increased population of all species but have all played a role in the other environmental issues. As wetlands are degraded or lost, many ecosystems and species will also be lost, interrupting their respective food webs. Food webs within the actual oceans will also be reduced due to pollution and climate changes that impact water temperatures and levels. The diminishment of coral reefs means the ocean's water filtration system will be reduced or totally destroyed, affecting the ecosystems themselves as well as the organisms that use the area for breeding and feeding.

30. A: The large intestine's main function is the reabsorption of water into the body to form solid waste. It also allows for the absorption of vitamin K produced by microbes living inside the large intestine.

31. D: Digestion of food in the small intestine occurs by bile secreted by the liver. This is a chemical change.

32. C: The opposite moon phase of a new moon is a full moon. A new moon is the first moon phase, followed by the first quarter and then the full moon. The last moon is not a moon phase.

33. D: Species may theoretically be able to inhabit a particular area, called its fundamental niche. But the presence of competing species may mean that it only occupies part of its niche, called a realized niche.

34. C: In plants, all eggs and sperm are produced by gametophytes. In mosses, the gametophyte is the most prominent stage. In angiosperms, gametophytes are tiny and found inside anthers and pistils.

35. A: A triple beam balance would be used to measure the mass (in grams) of the gum in this experiment. An anemometer is used to measure wind speed. A hot plate is used to heat liquids. A microscope is used to magnify microscopic particles or organisms.

36. B: All of the answers use the System of International Units (SI) of measurement with the exception of gallons. A liter is the measurement of a liquid. Grams are a unit of measurement for the weight of an object, which would be measured on the triple beam balance. Meters measure length.

37. D: Operons are common to prokaryotes. They are units of DNA that control the transcription of DNA and code for their own regulatory proteins as well as structural proteins.

38. C: The independent variable is the variable that is changed in the experiment in order to determine its effect on the dependent variable or the outcome of the experiment. The dependent variable results from the experimenter making only one change to an experiment that can be repeated with the same results. Mrs. Jones's class was comparing the effects of sugar and artificial sweetener on the overall color of cookies once they are baked; thus, the one thing that should be changed in the experiment is the sugar and artificial sweetener in the recipe. All of the other ingredients stay the same. For the experiment to be valid and not influenced by any other variables, the students should keep the temperature and baking time the same, as these could affect the color of the cookies as well.

39. B: A decrease in a natural predator, such as a wolves, coyotes, bobcat, or wild dogs, would allow the population to become out of control. In a population of deer that has increased, there would be a natural decrease in a food source for the nutritional needs for the animals. Although deer have been known to share a human's developed habitat, it is often forced by reduced territory and food sources. An increase in hunting licenses would be used by local officials to try to control the population, helping to decrease the number of adults of breeding age.

40. D: An independent variable is a variable in the experiment that is changed by the experimenter. In this experiment, the class changed the type of solution that was applied to each of the plants in order to determine which would provide the best overall color.

41. A: Salt would have acted as a dehydrating agent on the plants, causing them to dry out, and therefore, they would have died.

42. B: A control is a variable in the experiment that has not been changed by the experimenter but is subjected to the same processes as the other tested components. Plants are usually provided only water; these are being tested against bleach, salt, and diet soda, all of which are not regularly used to water a plant. The control acts as a reference point for comparison of the results,

43. D: A hypothesis is the use of prior knowledge in order to provide a hypothetical explanation for why something may or may not occur. A hypothesis can be proved wrong or right based on the results of the experiment and repeated trials.

44. C: In order to have accurate measurements, the use of a graduated cylinder would be best. A triple beam balance measures the weight of an object in grams. A flask and a test tube are used to contain a liquid while being heated or stored.

45. D: The first steps in a scientific investigation process involve asking a question about a problem and doing background research in order to determine if there is a valid reason for the question and whether it has been previously tested.

46. D: Although data from previous trials is important for the final lab report and results summary, it is not important for the current trial being tested. A final summary will incorporate all trial data results and observations in order to determine a final conclusion about the results. Temperature, color changes, and the production of a gas or odor indicate that a chemical change has occurred and should be recorded as an observation.

47. B: When working with flammable materials or an open flame, the accessible location of the fire blanket and extinguisher must be known in order to maintain safety. However, should the flames not go out immediately or spread too quickly, immediately leave the room and call 911. Close the door behind you in an effort to contain the fire.

48. C: The best graph to represent data from repeated trials of an experiment would be a line graph, as it would allow the viewer to see overlapping data without obstruction. The graph could be illustrated using different colors representing each trial or car, which would allow easy comparison.

49. B: The data tables compare the impact of the Northern and Southern Hemispheres on global warming with the overall changes globally, as seen in the top table. The Northern Hemisphere almost mirrors the results seen on the global table, while the Southern Hemisphere's table shows increases in temperature that are not as high as the Northern Hemispheres in years from 1980 to 2000. Most of the industrialized nations are found in the Northern Hemisphere. The Eastern and Western Hemispheres are not present on the table.

50. D: Blood is cooled as it passes through capillaries surrounding the sweat glands. Heat is absorbed along with excess salt and water and transferred to the glands as sweat. Droplets of sweat then evaporate from the skin surface to dissipate heat and cool the body. The kidney, bladder, and liver are not involved in regulating body temperature.

51. C: The most basic units of matter are protons, electrons, and neutrons. Protons are found in the nucleus, and have a positive charge. They are one of the three components of a helium atom a. When atoms have positive or negative charges, they are known as ions b. Molecules of oxygen, water, etc. d. are even more complex, consisting of one or more atoms held together by bonds.

52. D: Only cells with a membrane around the nucleus are called eukaryotes.

53. B: When Mario lets go of the book, he is no longer exerting any force on it, so he cannot be doing work on it. In all the other examples, Mario is exerting a force on the book in the direction that it is moving. In Answer A, Mario moves a book from the floor to the top shelf. Mario lifted up vertically on the book, in the same direction that the book moved, so he was doing work. In Answer C, Mario pushes a box of books across the room. This is also an example of work being done because the box moved in the direction of the force Mario applied. In Answer D, Mario is indirectly applying a horizontal force to the book because of the friction between the book and his head, so he is exerting a force on the book in the direction he is moving.

54. Third: All three laws are operating, but the third law (forces come in equal and opposite pairs) best explains the motion. The first law (inertia) is shown from the fact that the balloon doesn't move until a force acts upon it. The second law (F = ma) is shown because you can see the force and the acceleration. The force comes from the contraction of the rubber balloon. The stretched rubber exerts a force on the air inside the balloon. This causes the air to accelerate in accordance with the second law. You can't see this acceleration because the air is invisible and because it is all the air in the room that the balloon is exerting a force on. However, the air in the room exerts an equal and opposite force on the balloon (this is Newton's third law), which causes the balloon to accelerate in the direction it did.

How to Overcome Test Anxiety

Just the thought of taking a test is enough to make most people a little nervous. A test is an important event that can have a long-term impact on your future, so it's important to take it seriously and it's natural to feel anxious about performing well. But just because anxiety is normal, that doesn't mean that it's helpful in test taking, or that you should simply accept it as part of your life. Anxiety can have a variety of effects. These effects can be mild, like making you feel slightly nervous, or severe, like blocking your ability to focus or remember even a simple detail.

If you experience test anxiety—whether severe or mild—it's important to know how to beat it. To discover this, first you need to understand what causes test anxiety.

Causes of Test Anxiety

While we often think of anxiety as an uncontrollable emotional state, it can actually be caused by simple, practical things. One of the most common causes of test anxiety is that a person does not feel adequately prepared for their test. This feeling can be the result of many different issues such as poor study habits or lack of organization, but the most common culprit is time management. Starting to study too late, failing to organize your study time to cover all of the material, or being distracted while you study will mean that you're not well prepared for the test. This may lead to cramming the night before, which will cause you to be physically and mentally exhausted for the test. Poor time management also contributes to feelings of stress, fear, and hopelessness as you realize you are not well prepared but don't know what to do about it.

Other times, test anxiety is not related to your preparation for the test but comes from unresolved fear. This may be a past failure on a test, or poor performance on tests in general. It may come from comparing yourself to others who seem to be performing better or from the stress of living up to expectations. Anxiety may be driven by fears of the future—how failure on this test would affect your educational and career goals. These fears are often completely irrational, but they can still negatively impact your test performance.

> **Review Video:** 3 Reasons You Have Test Anxiety
> Visit mometrix.com/academy and enter code: 428468

Elements of Test Anxiety

As mentioned earlier, test anxiety is considered to be an emotional state, but it has physical and mental components as well. Sometimes you may not even realize that you are suffering from test anxiety until you notice the physical symptoms. These can include trembling hands, rapid heartbeat, sweating, nausea, and tense muscles. Extreme anxiety may lead to fainting or vomiting. Obviously, any of these symptoms can have a negative impact on testing. It is important to recognize them as soon as they begin to occur so that you can address the problem before it damages your performance.

> **Review Video:** 3 Ways to Tell You Have Test Anxiety
> Visit mometrix.com/academy and enter code: 927847

The mental components of test anxiety include trouble focusing and inability to remember learned information. During a test, your mind is on high alert, which can help you recall information and stay focused for an extended period of time. However, anxiety interferes with your mind's natural processes, causing you to blank out, even on the questions you know well. The strain of testing during anxiety makes it difficult to stay focused, especially on a test that may take several hours. Extreme anxiety can take a huge mental toll, making it difficult not only to recall test information but even to understand the test questions or pull your thoughts together.

> **Review Video:** How Test Anxiety Affects Memory
> Visit mometrix.com/academy and enter code: 609003

Effects of Test Anxiety

Test anxiety is like a disease—if left untreated, it will get progressively worse. Anxiety leads to poor performance, and this reinforces the feelings of fear and failure, which in turn lead to poor performances on subsequent tests. It can grow from a mild nervousness to a crippling condition. If allowed to progress, test anxiety can have a big impact on your schooling, and consequently on your future.

Test anxiety can spread to other parts of your life. Anxiety on tests can become anxiety in any stressful situation, and blanking on a test can turn into panicking in a job situation. But fortunately, you don't have to let anxiety rule your testing and determine your grades. There are a number of relatively simple steps you can take to move past anxiety and function normally on a test and in the rest of life.

> **Review Video:** How Test Anxiety Impacts Your Grades
> Visit mometrix.com/academy and enter code: 939819

Physical Steps for Beating Test Anxiety

While test anxiety is a serious problem, the good news is that it can be overcome. It doesn't have to control your ability to think and remember information. While it may take time, you can begin taking steps today to beat anxiety.

Just as your first hint that you may be struggling with anxiety comes from the physical symptoms, the first step to treating it is also physical. Rest is crucial for having a clear, strong mind. If you are tired, it is much easier to give in to anxiety. But if you establish good sleep habits, your body and mind will be ready to perform optimally, without the strain of exhaustion. Additionally, sleeping well helps you to retain information better, so you're more likely to recall the answers when you see the test questions.

Getting good sleep means more than going to bed on time. It's important to allow your brain time to relax. Take study breaks from time to time so it doesn't get overworked, and don't study right before bed. Take time to rest your mind before trying to rest your body, or you may find it difficult to fall asleep.

> **Review Video: The Importance of Sleep for Your Brain**
> Visit mometrix.com/academy and enter code: 319338

Along with sleep, other aspects of physical health are important in preparing for a test. Good nutrition is vital for good brain function. Sugary foods and drinks may give a burst of energy but this burst is followed by a crash, both physically and emotionally. Instead, fuel your body with protein and vitamin-rich foods.

Also, drink plenty of water. Dehydration can lead to headaches and exhaustion, especially if your brain is already under stress from the rigors of the test. Particularly if your test is a long one, drink water during the breaks. And if possible, take an energy-boosting snack to eat between sections.

> **Review Video: How Diet Can Affect your Mood**
> Visit mometrix.com/academy and enter code: 624317

Along with sleep and diet, a third important part of physical health is exercise. Maintaining a steady workout schedule is helpful, but even taking 5-minute study breaks to walk can help get your blood pumping faster and clear your head. Exercise also releases endorphins, which contribute to a positive feeling and can help combat test anxiety.

When you nurture your physical health, you are also contributing to your mental health. If your body is healthy, your mind is much more likely to be healthy as well. So take time to rest, nourish your body with healthy food and water, and get moving as much as possible. Taking these physical steps will make you stronger and more able to take the mental steps necessary to overcome test anxiety.

> **Review Video: How to Stay Healthy and Prevent Test Anxiety**
> Visit mometrix.com/academy and enter code: 877894

Mental Steps for Beating Test Anxiety

Working on the mental side of test anxiety can be more challenging, but as with the physical side, there are clear steps you can take to overcome it. As mentioned earlier, test anxiety often stems from lack of preparation, so the obvious solution is to prepare for the test. Effective studying may be the most important weapon you have for beating test anxiety, but you can and should employ several other mental tools to combat fear.

First, boost your confidence by reminding yourself of past success—tests or projects that you aced. If you're putting as much effort into preparing for this test as you did for those, there's no reason you should expect to fail here. Work hard to prepare; then trust your preparation.

Second, surround yourself with encouraging people. It can be helpful to find a study group, but be sure that the people you're around will encourage a positive attitude. If you spend time with others who are anxious or cynical, this will only contribute to your own anxiety. Look for others who are motivated to study hard from a desire to succeed, not from a fear of failure.

Third, reward yourself. A test is physically and mentally tiring, even without anxiety, and it can be helpful to have something to look forward to. Plan an activity following the test, regardless of the outcome, such as going to a movie or getting ice cream.

When you are taking the test, if you find yourself beginning to feel anxious, remind yourself that you know the material. Visualize successfully completing the test. Then take a few deep, relaxing breaths and return to it. Work through the questions carefully but with confidence, knowing that you are capable of succeeding.

Developing a healthy mental approach to test taking will also aid in other areas of life. Test anxiety affects more than just the actual test—it can be damaging to your mental health and even contribute to depression. It's important to beat test anxiety before it becomes a problem for more than testing.

> **Review Video: Test Anxiety and Depression**
> Visit mometrix.com/academy and enter code: 904704

Study Strategy

Being prepared for the test is necessary to combat anxiety, but what does being prepared look like? You may study for hours on end and still not feel prepared. What you need is a strategy for test prep. The next few pages outline our recommended steps to help you plan out and conquer the challenge of preparation.

Step 1: Scope Out the Test

Learn everything you can about the format (multiple choice, essay, etc.) and what will be on the test. Gather any study materials, course outlines, or sample exams that may be available. Not only will this help you to prepare, but knowing what to expect can help to alleviate test anxiety.

Step 2: Map Out the Material

Look through the textbook or study guide and make note of how many chapters or sections it has. Then divide these over the time you have. For example, if a book has 15 chapters and you have five days to study, you need to cover three chapters each day. Even better, if you have the time, leave an extra day at the end for overall review after you have gone through the material in depth.

If time is limited, you may need to prioritize the material. Look through it and make note of which sections you think you already have a good grasp on, and which need review. While you are studying, skim quickly through the familiar sections and take more time on the challenging parts. Write out your plan so you don't get lost as you go. Having a written plan also helps you feel more in control of the study, so anxiety is less likely to arise from feeling overwhelmed at the amount to cover. A sample plan may look like this:

- Day 1: Skim chapters 1–4, study chapter 5 (especially pages 31–33)
- Day 2: Study chapters 6–7, skim chapters 8–9
- Day 3: Skim chapter 10, study chapters 11–12 (especially pages 87–90)
- Day 4: Study chapters 13–15
- Day 5: Overall review (focus most on chapters 5, 6, and 12), take practice test

Step 3: Gather Your Tools

Decide what study method works best for you. Do you prefer to highlight in the book as you study and then go back over the highlighted portions? Or do you type out notes of the important information? Or is it helpful to make flashcards that you can carry with you? Assemble the pens, index cards, highlighters, post-it notes, and any other materials you may need so you won't be distracted by getting up to find things while you study.

If you're having a hard time retaining the information or organizing your notes, experiment with different methods. For example, try color-coding by subject with colored pens, highlighters, or post-it notes. If you learn better by hearing, try recording yourself reading your notes so you can listen while in the car, working out, or simply sitting at your desk. Ask a friend to quiz you from your flashcards, or try teaching someone the material to solidify it in your mind.

Step 4: Create Your Environment

It's important to avoid distractions while you study. This includes both the obvious distractions like visitors and the subtle distractions like an uncomfortable chair (or a too-comfortable couch that makes you want to fall asleep). Set up the best study environment possible: good lighting and a comfortable work area. If background music helps you focus, you may want to turn it on, but otherwise keep the room quiet. If you are using a computer to take notes, be sure you don't have any other windows open, especially applications like social media, games, or anything else that could distract you. Silence your phone and turn off notifications. Be sure to keep water close by so you stay hydrated while you study (but avoid unhealthy drinks and snacks).

Also, take into account the best time of day to study. Are you freshest first thing in the morning? Try to set aside some time then to work through the material. Is your mind clearer in the afternoon or evening? Schedule your study session then. Another method is to study at the same time of day that you will take the test, so that your brain gets used to working on the material at that time and will be ready to focus at test time.

Step 5: Study!

Once you have done all the study preparation, it's time to settle into the actual studying. Sit down, take a few moments to settle your mind so you can focus, and begin to follow your study plan. Don't give in to distractions or let yourself procrastinate. This is your time to prepare so you'll be ready to fearlessly approach the test. Make the most of the time and stay focused.

Of course, you don't want to burn out. If you study too long you may find that you're not retaining the information very well. Take regular study breaks. For example, taking five minutes out of every hour to walk briskly, breathing deeply and swinging your arms, can help your mind stay fresh.

As you get to the end of each chapter or section, it's a good idea to do a quick review. Remind yourself of what you learned and work on any difficult parts. When you feel that you've mastered the material, move on to the next part. At the end of your study session, briefly skim through your notes again.

But while review is helpful, cramming last minute is NOT. If at all possible, work ahead so that you won't need to fit all your study into the last day. Cramming overloads your brain with more information than it can process and retain, and your tired mind may struggle to recall even previously learned information when it is overwhelmed with last-minute study. Also, the urgent nature of cramming and the stress placed on your brain contribute to anxiety. You'll be more likely to go to the test feeling unprepared and having trouble thinking clearly.

So don't cram, and don't stay up late before the test, even just to review your notes at a leisurely pace. Your brain needs rest more than it needs to go over the information again. In fact, plan to finish your studies by noon or early afternoon the day before the test. Give your brain the rest of the day to relax or focus on other things, and get a good night's sleep. Then you will be fresh for the test and better able to recall what you've studied.

Step 6: Take a practice test

Many courses offer sample tests, either online or in the study materials. This is an excellent resource to check whether you have mastered the material, as well as to prepare for the test format and environment.

Check the test format ahead of time: the number of questions, the type (multiple choice, free response, etc.), and the time limit. Then create a plan for working through them. For example, if you have 30 minutes to take a 60-question test, your limit is 30 seconds per question. Spend less time on the questions you know well so that you can take more time on the difficult ones.

If you have time to take several practice tests, take the first one open book, with no time limit. Work through the questions at your own pace and make sure you fully understand them. Gradually work up to taking a test under test conditions: sit at a desk with all study materials put away and set a timer. Pace yourself to make sure you finish the test with time to spare and go back to check your answers if you have time.

After each test, check your answers. On the questions you missed, be sure you understand why you missed them. Did you misread the question (tests can use tricky wording)? Did you forget the information? Or was it something you hadn't learned? Go back and study any shaky areas that the practice tests reveal.

Taking these tests not only helps with your grade, but also aids in combating test anxiety. If you're already used to the test conditions, you're less likely to worry about it, and working through tests until you're scoring well gives you a confidence boost. Go through the practice tests until you feel comfortable, and then you can go into the test knowing that you're ready for it.

Test Tips

On test day, you should be confident, knowing that you've prepared well and are ready to answer the questions. But aside from preparation, there are several test day strategies you can employ to maximize your performance.

First, as stated before, get a good night's sleep the night before the test (and for several nights before that, if possible). Go into the test with a fresh, alert mind rather than staying up late to study.

Try not to change too much about your normal routine on the day of the test. It's important to eat a nutritious breakfast, but if you normally don't eat breakfast at all, consider eating just a protein bar. If you're a coffee drinker, go ahead and have your normal coffee. Just make sure you time it so that the caffeine doesn't wear off right in the middle of your test. Avoid sugary beverages, and drink enough water to stay hydrated but not so much that you need a restroom break 10 minutes into the test. If your test isn't first thing in the morning, consider going for a walk or doing a light workout before the test to get your blood flowing.

Allow yourself enough time to get ready, and leave for the test with plenty of time to spare so you won't have the anxiety of scrambling to arrive in time. Another reason to be early is to select a good seat. It's helpful to sit away from doors and windows, which can be distracting. Find a good seat, get out your supplies, and settle your mind before the test begins.

When the test begins, start by going over the instructions carefully, even if you already know what to expect. Make sure you avoid any careless mistakes by following the directions.

Then begin working through the questions, pacing yourself as you've practiced. If you're not sure on an answer, don't spend too much time on it, and don't let it shake your confidence. Either skip it and come back later, or eliminate as many wrong answers as possible and guess among the remaining ones. Don't dwell on these questions as you continue—put them out of your mind and focus on what lies ahead.

Be sure to read all of the answer choices, even if you're sure the first one is the right answer. Sometimes you'll find a better one if you keep reading. But don't second-guess yourself if you do immediately know the answer. Your gut instinct is usually right. Don't let test anxiety rob you of the information you know.

If you have time at the end of the test (and if the test format allows), go back and review your answers. Be cautious about changing any, since your first instinct tends to be correct, but make sure you didn't misread any of the questions or accidentally mark the wrong answer choice. Look over any you skipped and make an educated guess.

At the end, leave the test feeling confident. You've done your best, so don't waste time worrying about your performance or wishing you could change anything. Instead, celebrate the successful completion of this test. And finally, use this test to learn how to deal with anxiety even better next time.

> **Review Video:** 5 Tips to Beat Test Anxiety
> Visit mometrix.com/academy and enter code: 570656

Important Qualification

Not all anxiety is created equal. If your test anxiety is causing major issues in your life beyond the classroom or testing center, or if you are experiencing troubling physical symptoms related to your anxiety, it may be a sign of a serious physiological or psychological condition. If this sounds like your situation, we strongly encourage you to seek professional help.

How to Overcome Your Fear of Math

The word *math* is enough to strike fear into most hearts. How many of us have memories of sitting through confusing lectures, wrestling over mind-numbing homework, or taking tests that still seem incomprehensible even after hours of study? Years after graduation, many still shudder at these memories.

The fact is, math is not just a classroom subject. It has real-world implications that you face every day, whether you realize it or not. This may be balancing your monthly budget, deciding how many supplies to buy for a project, or simply splitting a meal check with friends. The idea of daily confrontations with math can be so paralyzing that some develop a condition known as *math anxiety*.

But you do NOT need to be paralyzed by this anxiety! In fact, while you may have thought all your life that you're not good at math, or that your brain isn't wired to understand it, the truth is that you may have been conditioned to think this way. From your earliest school days, the way you were taught affected the way you viewed different subjects. And the way math has been taught has changed.

Several decades ago, there was a shift in American math classrooms. The focus changed from traditional problem-solving to a conceptual view of topics, de-emphasizing the importance of learning the basics and building on them. The solid foundation necessary for math progression and confidence was undermined. Math became more of a vague concept than a concrete idea. Today, it is common to think of math, not as a straightforward system, but as a mysterious, complicated method that can't be fully understood unless you're a genius.

This is why you may still have nightmares about being called on to answer a difficult problem in front of the class. Math anxiety is a very real, though unnecessary, fear.

Math anxiety may begin with a single class period. Let's say you missed a day in 6th grade math and never quite understood the concept that was taught while you were gone. Since math is cumulative, with each new concept building on past ones, this could very well affect the rest of your math career. Without that one day's knowledge, it will be difficult to understand any other concepts that link to it. Rather than realizing that you're just missing one key piece, you may begin to believe that you're simply not capable of understanding math.

This belief can change the way you approach other classes, career options, and everyday life experiences, if you become anxious at the thought that math might be required. A student who loves science may choose a different path of study upon realizing that multiple math classes will be required for a degree. An aspiring medical student may hesitate at the thought of going through the necessary math classes. For some this anxiety escalates into a more extreme state known as *math phobia*.

Math anxiety is challenging to address because it is rooted deeply and may come from a variety of causes: an embarrassing moment in class, a teacher who did not explain concepts well and contributed to a shaky foundation, or a failed test that contributed to the belief of math failure.

These causes add up over time, encouraged by society's popular view that math is hard and unpleasant. Eventually a person comes to firmly believe that he or she is simply bad at math. This belief makes it difficult to grasp new concepts or even remember old ones. Homework and test grades begin to slip, which only confirms the belief. The poor performance is not due to lack of ability but is caused by math anxiety.

Math anxiety is an emotional issue, not a lack of intelligence. But when it becomes deeply rooted, it can become more than just an emotional problem. Physical symptoms appear. Blood pressure may rise and heartbeat may quicken at the sight of a math problem – or even the thought of math! This fear leads to a mental block. When someone with math anxiety is asked to perform a calculation, even a basic problem can seem overwhelming and impossible. The emotional and physical response to the thought of math prevents the brain from working through it logically.

The more this happens, the more a person's confidence drops, and the more math anxiety is generated. This vicious cycle must be broken!

The first step in breaking the cycle is to go back to very beginning and make sure you really understand the basics of how math works and why it works. It is not enough to memorize rules for multiplication and division. If you don't know WHY these rules work, your foundation will be shaky and you will be at risk of developing a phobia. Understanding mathematical concepts not only promotes confidence and security, but allows you to build on this understanding for new concepts. Additionally, you can solve unfamiliar problems using familiar concepts and processes.

Why is it that students in other countries regularly outperform American students in math? The answer likely boils down to a couple of things: the foundation of mathematical conceptual understanding and societal perception. While students in the US are not expected to *like* or *get* math, in many other nations, students are expected not only to understand math but also to excel at it.

Changing the American view of math that leads to math anxiety is a monumental task. It requires changing the training of teachers nationwide, from kindergarten through high school, so that they learn to teach the *why* behind math and to combat the wrong math views that students may develop. It also involves changing the stigma associated with math, so that it is no longer viewed as unpleasant and incomprehensible. While these are necessary changes, they are challenging and will take time. But in the meantime, math anxiety is not irreversible—it can be faced and defeated, one person at a time.

False Beliefs

One reason math anxiety has taken such hold is that several false beliefs have been created and shared until they became widely accepted. Some of these unhelpful beliefs include the following:

There is only one way to solve a math problem. In the same way that you can choose from different driving routes and still arrive at the same house, you can solve a math problem using different methods and still find the correct answer. A person who understands the reasoning behind math calculations may be able to look at an unfamiliar concept and find the right answer, just by applying logic to the knowledge they already have. This approach may be different than what is taught in the classroom, but it is still valid. Unfortunately, even many teachers view math as a subject where the best course of action is to memorize the rule or process for each problem rather than as a place for students to exercise logic and creativity in finding a solution.

Many people don't have a mind for math. A person who has struggled due to poor teaching or math anxiety may falsely believe that he or she doesn't have the mental capacity to grasp mathematical concepts. Most of the time, this is false. Many people find that when they are relieved of their math anxiety, they have more than enough brainpower to understand math.

Men are naturally better at math than women. Even though research has shown this to be false, many young women still avoid math careers and classes because of their belief that their math abilities are inferior. Many girls have come to believe that math is a male skill and have given up trying to understand or enjoy it.

Counting aids are bad. Something like counting on your fingers or drawing out a problem to visualize it may be frowned on as childish or a crutch, but these devices can help you get a tangible understanding of a problem or a concept.

Sadly, many students buy into these ideologies at an early age. A young girl who enjoys math class may be conditioned to think that she doesn't actually have the brain for it because math is for boys, and may turn her energies to other pursuits, permanently closing the door on a wide range of opportunities. A child who finds the right answer but doesn't follow the teacher's method may believe that he is doing it wrong and isn't good at math. A student who never had a problem with math before may have a poor teacher and become confused, yet believe that the problem is because she doesn't have a mathematical mind.

Students who have bought into these erroneous beliefs quickly begin to add their own anxieties, adapting them to their own personal situations:

I'll never use this in real life. A huge number of people wrongly believe that math is irrelevant outside the classroom. By adopting this mindset, they are handicapping themselves for a life in a mathematical world, as well as limiting their career choices. When they are inevitably faced with real-world math, they are conditioning themselves to respond with anxiety.

I'm not quick enough. While timed tests and quizzes, or even simply comparing yourself with other students in the class, can lead to this belief, speed is not an indicator of skill level. A person can work very slowly yet understand at a deep level.

If I can understand it, it's too easy. People with a low view of their own abilities tend to think that if they are able to grasp a concept, it must be simple. They cannot accept the idea that they are capable of understanding math. This belief will make it harder to learn, no matter how intelligent they are.

I just can't learn this. An overwhelming number of people think this, from young children to adults, and much of the time it is simply not true. But this mindset can turn into a self-fulfilling prophecy that keeps you from exercising and growing your math ability.

The good news is, each of these myths can be debunked. For most people, they are based on emotion and psychology, NOT on actual ability! It will take time, effort, and the desire to change, but change is possible. Even if you have spent years thinking that you don't have the capability to understand math, it is not too late to uncover your true ability and find relief from the anxiety that surrounds math.

Math Strategies

It is important to have a plan of attack to combat math anxiety. There are many useful strategies for pinpointing the fears or myths and eradicating them:

Go back to the basics. For most people, math anxiety stems from a poor foundation. You may think that you have a complete understanding of addition and subtraction, or even decimals and percentages, but make absolutely sure. Learning math is different from learning other subjects. For example, when you learn history, you study various time periods and places and events. It may be important to memorize dates or find out about the lives of famous people. When you move from US history to world history, there will be some overlap, but a large amount of the information will be new. Mathematical concepts, on the other hand, are very closely linked and highly dependent on each other. It's like climbing a ladder – if a rung is missing from your understanding, it may be difficult or impossible for you to climb any higher, no matter how hard you try. So go back and make sure your math foundation is strong. This may mean taking a remedial math course, going to a tutor to work through the shaky concepts, or just going through your old homework to make sure you really understand it.

Speak the language. Math has a large vocabulary of terms and phrases unique to working problems. Sometimes these are completely new terms, and sometimes they are common words, but are used differently in a math setting. If you can't speak the language, it will be very difficult to get a thorough understanding of the concepts. It's common for students to think that they don't understand math when they simply don't understand the vocabulary. The good news is that this is fairly easy to fix. Brushing up on any terms you aren't quite sure of can help bring the rest of the concepts into focus.

Check your anxiety level. When you think about math, do you feel nervous or uncomfortable? Do you struggle with feelings of inadequacy, even on concepts that you know you've already learned? It's important to understand your specific math anxieties, and what triggers them. When you catch yourself falling back on a false belief, mentally replace it with the truth. Don't let yourself believe that you can't learn, or that struggling with a concept means you'll never understand it. Instead, remind yourself of how much you've already learned and dwell on that past success. Visualize grasping the new concept, linking it to your old knowledge, and moving on to the next challenge. Also, learn how to manage anxiety when it arises. There are many techniques for coping with the irrational fears that rise to the surface when you enter the math classroom. This may include controlled breathing, replacing negative thoughts with positive ones, or visualizing success. Anxiety interferes with your ability to concentrate and absorb information, which in turn contributes to greater anxiety. If you can learn how to regain control of your thinking, you will be better able to pay attention, make progress, and succeed!

Don't go it alone. Like any deeply ingrained belief, math anxiety is not easy to eradicate. And there is no need for you to wrestle through it on your own. It will take time, and many people find that speaking with a counselor or psychiatrist helps. They can help you develop strategies for responding to anxiety and overcoming old ideas. Additionally, it can be very helpful to take a short course or seek out a math tutor to help you find and fix the missing rungs on your ladder and make sure that you're ready to progress to the next level. You can also find a number of math aids online: courses that will teach you mental devices for figuring out problems, how to get the most out of your math classes, etc.

Check your math attitude. No matter how much you want to learn and overcome your anxiety, you'll have trouble if you still have a negative attitude toward math. If you think it's too hard, or just

- 84 -

have general feelings of dread about math, it will be hard to learn and to break through the anxiety. Work on cultivating a positive math attitude. Remind yourself that math is not just a hurdle to be cleared, but a valuable asset. When you view math with a positive attitude, you'll be much more likely to understand and even enjoy it. This is something you must do for yourself. You may find it helpful to visit with a counselor. Your tutor, friends, and family may cheer you on in your endeavors. But your greatest asset is yourself. You are inside your own mind – tell yourself what you need to hear. Relive past victories. Remind yourself that you are capable of understanding math. Root out any false beliefs that linger and replace them with positive truths. Even if it doesn't feel true at first, it will begin to affect your thinking and pave the way for a positive, anxiety-free mindset.

Aside from these general strategies, there are a number of specific practical things you can do to begin your journey toward overcoming math anxiety. Something as simple as learning a new note-taking strategy can change the way you approach math and give you more confidence and understanding. New study techniques can also make a huge difference.

Math anxiety leads to bad habits. If it causes you to be afraid of answering a question in class, you may gravitate toward the back row. You may be embarrassed to ask for help. And you may procrastinate on assignments, which leads to rushing through them at the last moment when it's too late to get a better understanding. It's important to identify your negative behaviors and replace them with positive ones:

Prepare ahead of time. Read the lesson before you go to class. Being exposed to the topics that will be covered in class ahead of time, even if you don't understand them perfectly, is extremely helpful in increasing what you retain from the lecture. Do your homework and, if you're still shaky, go over some extra problems. The key to a solid understanding of math is practice.

Sit front and center. When you can easily see and hear, you'll understand more, and you'll avoid the distractions of other students if no one is in front of you. Plus, you're more likely to be sitting with students who are positive and engaged, rather than others with math anxiety. Let their positive math attitude rub off on you.

Ask questions in class and out. If you don't understand something, just ask. If you need a more in-depth explanation, the teacher may need to work with you outside of class, but often it's a simple concept you don't quite understand, and a single question may clear it up. If you wait, you may not be able to follow the rest of the day's lesson. For extra help, most professors have office hours outside of class when you can go over concepts one-on-one to clear up any uncertainties. Additionally, there may be a *math lab* or study session you can attend for homework help. Take advantage of this.

Review. Even if you feel that you've fully mastered a concept, review it periodically to reinforce it. Going over an old lesson has several benefits: solidifying your understanding, giving you a confidence boost, and even giving some new insights into material that you're currently learning! Don't let yourself get rusty. That can lead to problems with learning later concepts.

Teaching Tips

While the math student's mindset is the most crucial to overcoming math anxiety, it is also important for others to adjust their math attitudes. Teachers and parents have an enormous influence on how students relate to math. They can either contribute to math confidence or math anxiety.

As a parent or teacher, it is very important to convey a positive math attitude. Retelling horror stories of your own bad experience with math will contribute to a new generation of math anxiety. Even if you don't share your experiences, others will be able to sense your fears and may begin to believe them.

Even a careless comment can have a big impact, so watch for phrases like *He's not good at math* or *I never liked math*. You are a crucial role model, and your children or students will unconsciously adopt your mindset. Give them a positive example to follow. Rather than teaching them to fear the math world before they even know it, teach them about all its potential and excitement.

Work to present math as an integral, beautiful, and understandable part of life. Encourage creativity in solving problems. Watch for false beliefs and dispel them. Cross the lines between subjects: integrate history, English, and music with math. Show students how math is used every day, and how the entire world is based on mathematical principles, from the pull of gravity to the shape of seashells. Instead of letting students see math as a necessary evil, direct them to view it as an imaginative, beautiful art form – an art form that they are capable of mastering and using.

Don't give too narrow a view of math. It is more than just numbers. Yes, working problems and learning formulas is a large part of classroom math. But don't let the teaching stop there. Teach students about the everyday implications of math. Show them how nature works according to the laws of mathematics, and take them outside to make discoveries of their own. Expose them to math-related careers by inviting visiting speakers, asking students to do research and presentations, and learning students' interests and aptitudes on a personal level.

Demonstrate the importance of math. Many people see math as nothing more than a required stepping stone to their degree, a nuisance with no real usefulness. Teach students that algebra is used every day in managing their bank accounts, in following recipes, and in scheduling the day's events. Show them how learning to do geometric proofs helps them to develop logical thinking, an invaluable life skill. Let them see that math surrounds them and is integrally linked to their daily lives: that weather predictions are based on math, that math was used to design cars and other machines, etc. Most of all, give them the tools to use math to enrich their lives.

Make math as tangible as possible. Use visual aids and objects that can be touched. It is much easier to grasp a concept when you can hold it in your hands and manipulate it, rather than just listening to the lecture. Encourage math outside of the classroom. The real world is full of measuring, counting, and calculating, so let students participate in this. Keep your eyes open for numbers and patterns to discuss. Talk about how scores are calculated in sports games and how far apart plants are placed in a garden row for maximum growth. Build the mindset that math is a normal and interesting part of daily life.

Finally, find math resources that help to build a positive math attitude. There are a number of books that show math as fascinating and exciting while teaching important concepts, for example: *The Math Curse; A Wrinkle in Time; The Phantom Tollbooth;* and *Fractals, Googols and Other Mathematical Tales*. You can also find a number of online resources: math puzzles and games, videos that show math in nature, and communities of math enthusiasts. On a local level, students can compete in a variety of math competitions with other schools or join a math club.

The student who experiences math as exciting and interesting is unlikely to suffer from math anxiety. Going through life without this handicap is an immense advantage and opens many doors that others have closed through their fear.

Self-Check

Whether you suffer from math anxiety or not, chances are that you have been exposed to some of the false beliefs mentioned above. Now is the time to check yourself for any errors you may have accepted. Do you think you're not wired for math? Or that you don't need to understand it since you're not planning on a math career? Do you think math is just too difficult for the average person?

Find the errors you've taken to heart and replace them with positive thinking. Are you capable of learning math? Yes! Can you control your anxiety? Yes! These errors will resurface from time to time, so be watchful. Don't let others with math anxiety influence you or sway your confidence. If you're having trouble with a concept, find help. Don't let it discourage you!

Create a plan of attack for defeating math anxiety and sharpening your skills. Do some research and decide if it would help you to take a class, get a tutor, or find some online resources to fine-tune your knowledge. Make the effort to get good nutrition, hydration, and sleep so that you are operating at full capacity. Remind yourself daily that you are skilled and that anxiety does not control you. Your mind is capable of so much more than you know. Give it the tools it needs to grow and thrive.

Thank You

We at Mometrix would like to extend our heartfelt thanks to you, our friend and patron, for allowing us to play a part in your journey. It is a privilege to serve people from all walks of life who are unified in their commitment to building the best future they can for themselves.

The preparation you devote to these important testing milestones may be the most valuable educational opportunity you have for making a real difference in your life. We encourage you to put your heart into it—that feeling of succeeding, overcoming, and yes, conquering will be well worth the hours you've invested.

We want to hear your story, your struggles and your successes, and if you see any opportunities for us to improve our materials so we can help others even more effectively in the future, please share that with us as well. **The team at Mometrix would be absolutely thrilled to hear from you!** So please, send us an email (support@mometrix.com) and let's stay in touch.

If you'd like some additional help, check out these other resources we offer for your exam:

http://mometrixflashcards.com/FSA

Additional Bonus Material

Due to our efforts to try to keep this book to a manageable length, we've created a link that will give you access to all of your additional bonus material.

Please visit http://www.mometrix.com/bonus948/fsag8sci to access the information.